CELEBRATING

THE

12 DAYS OF CHRISTMAS

CELEBRATING THE 12 DAYS of CHRISTMAS

CELEBRATING

THE

12 DAYS OF CHRISTMAS

A Guide for Churches and Families

CHRIS MARCHAND

ILLUSTRATIONS BY BLAIR E. CLARK

WIPF & STOCK · Eugene, Oregon

CELEBRATING THE 12 DAYS OF CHRISTMAS
A Guide for Churches and Families

Wipf and Stock
An Imprint of Wipf and Stock Publishers
199 W. 8th Ave., Suite 3
Eugene, OR 97401

www.wipfandstock.com

PAPERBACK ISBN: 978-1-5326-5533-3
HARDCOVER ISBN: 978-1-5326-5534-0
EBOOK ISBN: 978-1-5326-5535-7

Manufactured in the U.S.A.   10/02/19

To my children Elliot, Micah, Isaac, and Shiloh.
To your children too, and their children's children.
"The true meaning of life is to plant trees under whose shade you do not expect to sit."

—NELSON HENDERSON

Contents

Acknowledgments

ODDLY ENOUGH, THIS BOOK would not have gotten written if years ago Fernando Ortega had not responded to a set of interview questions I slapdashedly left in the comments of an article he wrote on his website. He *did* respond to those questions and it has given me the courage and audacity to keep on writing in the hope that people might actually pay attention to it. So thank you, sir. This book also would not have gotten written were it not for an interview Bishop Keith Ackerman did surrounding the traditions of the 12 days of Christmas (Fr. Don Sackett and Fr. Tom Janikowski were the interviewers). The insights and suggestions Bishop Ackerman shared there hit me to such an extent that I could only exclaim, "Nobody knows these things! There needs to be a book written about it!" This realization led me on the path to contact Bishop Ackerman, and after finding out he did not want to co-write the book with me, I decided that I should take on the project myself. I want to thank the bishop for the time he took to discuss Christmas with me, as well as *all* of those I interviewed in research for the book: Dr. Michael Ward, Dr. Susan K. Roll, Dr. E. Byron Anderson, Michelle Van Loon, Gretchen Filz, Bishop Alberto Morales, Fr. Andrew Kishler, Tyler Swartzentruber, Gabi and Petr Michlik, and Eliana Agness. I must specifically lift up Petr Michlik, whom I have had numerous conversations with (dare I say quarrels?) surrounding the "corrupted" origins of Christmas. Those many conversations caused me to truly want to get to the bottom of things about this conflicting holiday. Indeed, this book would not have gotten written without you.

I next need to thank the many people who over the years have taught and encouraged me to write, research, think, and read texts well: Dr. E. Byron Anderson (the work you did on my masters thesis will always be an honor to me), Dr. Kathy Whitson, Dr. D. Stephen Long, Dr. George

Kalantzis, Dr. Brent Waters, Professor Mike Foster, Dr. Ann McClellan, Carole Ronane, and Dr. Joseph Yao-Kotay. And thank you to the numerous friends who have been my conversation partners—the "work" we did through talking things out has shaped me into the writer and thinker I am: Brandon Lulay, Rev. Dan Leman, Fr. Greg Lynn, Dr. Ben Sutton, Fr. Eric Speece, Rev. Dr. Jeremiah Gibbs, Deacon Amanda Holm-Rosengren, and Rev. Jay Greener.

Blair, thanks for your art—the work you did is incredible and I hope people can see the layers of meaning. I also hope people are challenged by your images in the same way that they are challenged by my words. Seth, thank you for generously putting together my promo video—now let's go get some coffee. Brandon, thanks for the pre-edit—I'd offer to return the favor someday, but I know I wouldn't do half as good a job. You are my brother and I'm so grateful for you. And thanks to anyone who supported or promoted the Kickstarter campaign to fund this book.

Finally, thank you to my wife and my mother. Elisa, thank you for the time to write and for reading through and editing so much of it. I hope it turned out ok. Mom, thank you for the years of constant encouragement. Hopefully all those uplifting words have finally turned into something tangible.

I essentially wrote this book for my children, Elliot, Micah, Isaac, and Shiloh, a legacy who will endure far beyond myself. One day you will grow up and realize that yes, dad did in fact write a book, and my hope is you will take time to mine the treasures in these pages and consider what virtues and beauties they might bring to your own lives and the communities in which you live. May we all continue to make a pilgrimage to Christ each Christmas, being able to proclaim in worship together, "Christ is born! He is born indeed! Alleluia!"

Introduction

The Most Wonderful Time of the Year?

CHRISTMAS IS A SPECIAL time of year. It is a time where people come together and celebrate the love we have for each other. It is a time of warm hearths, gorgeous music, grandma's cookies, colorful decorations, and the giving of heartfelt gifts. Christmas is the time of year when we slow down and are thankful for all of God's blessings—for God's provision throughout the past year, but most especially for the coming of God's Son, our savior.

Oh who are we kidding? Most of us barely have enough time throughout the "Christmas Season" to think about any of those good things. Instead, we are frenzied, rushed, and continually worried about making *this* year an "extra special Christmas." We are *caught up* for sure, but most often it seems we are caught up in the *wrong* things. There is the pressure to buy numerous "perfect" gifts. There is the dread of having to celebrate the holidays through a string of seemingly endless parties with various friends and family members whom we rarely see anymore and with whom we have very little in common. For young families there is the exhaustingly stressful grind of carting our children around from shopping malls, to church services, to various relatives' houses. And for some of us there is the empty ache of having nowhere to go at all and no one who wants to see us—in other words, the holidays are an incredibly isolated and lonely time, a reminder of how alone we are.

But is this Christmas as it *should* be? Nearly all of us would acknowledge it is not, but we hardly have any experiences or resources with which to guide us into a different way of *doing* Christmas. Instead, we are locked into a seemingly inescapable civic calendar of buying as much as possible from Thanksgiving until Christmas Eve, decorating the inside and outside of our home, having various work, school, and church parties, taking part in or attending various Christmas productions and concerts, going to church on Christmas Eve or Morning, opening presents on Christmas Eve or Morning, going to someone's house on Christmas Day, and finally lying around the house until New Year's because we are all so exhausted, bloated, and overwhelmed by the influx of gifts and toys. Does that sound like *your* "Christmas Season"?

In the wake of the hectic busyness of "the most wonderful time of the year" many of us are silently left asking: "Is there another way to *do* Christmas? And if there *is* a way, can anyone give us a guide on what it should look like?" This book is an attempt to answer those questions and offer the requested guide. Its inception began years ago with a few incessant, nagging questions that popped into my mind just about every December: "What exactly are the 12 days of Christmas anyway? Do they actually exist and does anybody actually celebrate them? Because I certainly don't know anybody who does." In part, these questions arose from yearly listens to the carol "The Twelve Days of Christmas." The song itself is something of an inexplicable anomaly: it contains lyrics no one knows the meaning of and references a ritual that no one practices (the 12 days), and yet it persists as a staple of the season.

Though unpacking the basic meaning of the 12-day season and its accompanying carol was a mere article away, I never really pursued it further. The unanswered dissonance evaporated into the busyness of adult life: there was too much to *do* for Christmas to actually take time to look up what I should actually *be doing* during Christmas. Thankfully and unexpectedly some answers made their way to me, but not before my faith took on an entirely new shape over the course of a number of years. After growing up in the Pentecostal–Evangelical tradition, I became an Anglican over a decade ago while on a search for a deeper, more ancient practice of Christianity. I was enthralled to learn about the beauty of ritual in the liturgy and how God draws near to us physically and spiritually in the sacraments. I immersed myself in "the faith once delivered," learning what it meant to follow the ancient paths while still holding the Scriptures as my ultimate foundation. Every season of the year felt utterly transformed: Advent, Lent, Easter, and Ordinary Time came alive in fullness.

But not so with Christmas. Even though the *meaning* of it had deepened in my understanding of why Christ came to earth, Christmas was mostly the same *in practice*: go to a few church services, open presents, and . . . that's about it. "Christmas" still felt too secular and compartmentalized, as if "over here I'm going to do some *spiritual* Christmassy things, over here I'm going to do some *consumerist* Christmassy things, and over *here* I'm going to do some *family-oriented* Christmassy things." I was left wondering: "Is there a way I can do Christmas so that *all* of it feels sacred and set apart as holy unto the Lord?"

In the midst of this Christmas desert wandering I heard Bishop Keith Ackerman on an Anglican podcast (produced by a few priests within my diocese). They interviewed him about ways to celebrate the full Christmas season. For the first time in my life the celebration of Christmas itself came alive to me in awakening fullness, but I needed someone to show me and tell me how to do it, to model it in front of me. For this reason, I contacted Bishop Ackerman and conducted a couple of lengthy interviews with him. I got to ask him numerous questions and he got to lay out his passionate vision of what the Christmas season can become for the body of Christ. This book originated out of my own lack of knowledge and a desire to know "a more excellent way" (1 Cor 12:31). My hope is that it can provide a framework for others as well.

I am Anglican, so doing Christmas the "traditional" way and according to the Church calendar should be somewhat easy for me (even though it still takes a lot of counter-cultural effort!); but my main hope in writing this book is to show how *all* Christians can live into the fullness of the season, that is, the 12 Days, which begins on December 25 and culminates with Epiphany on January 6. I realize looking at changing *how* we celebrate Christmas can be a daunting task. But rather than scaring other Christians away from this holy season, my aim is to give us all a beautiful vision of what doing Christmas a new way can look like, which just so happens to be a very *old* way.

This book is about understanding the meaning and history behind the Christmas holy days and then about knowing how those days should be celebrated. It is about worshipping together, celebrating together, and serving our world together in the name of Christ who has come to save us. Therefore, it is essentially about being a better disciple of Jesus and allowing our beliefs about Jesus to spur us into action in word and deed. At Christmas, we proclaim the coming of Christ in *word* by reading the narratives in the Gospels of Luke and Matthew and John, but we show the world who Christ is in *deed* by how we live out together the good news of his coming.

With all this in mind, the book takes on a straightforward structure: after tackling a number of misconceptions and frequently asked questions about Christmas in chapter 1, chapter 2 explains the meanings of Advent, Christmas, and Epiphany and how they go together. Then in the remaining chapters I lay out a day-by-day description of the different feast days and holy days the Church can enter into during the 12-day season (including a chapter on pre-Christmas traditions). The first half of each chapter describes the meaning and background of each day, and the second half lays out practical suggestions for how to worship and celebrate on those days.

So what is the Christmas season all about and how should it be celebrated? Broken down to essentials, all our various traditions fit into four intersecting categories:

- Worshipping with the people of God.
- Leisure through celebrations with gathered friends and family
- Serving those around us in need.
- Leisure through resting

All the practical suggestions in this book for incorporating new rituals and celebrations into your Christmas season use the above categories as their basis. But it should be noted: the "12 days of Christmas" is not about 12 days of unending celebration. Thankfully, each of the 12 days is not usually taken up with it's own feast day or holy day, but instead only six of the days if you count Christmas Day and Epiphany. Thus, a lot of restful downtime is implied in the 12 days. There are days or segments of days devoted to worship, prayer, and reflection, days devoted to community celebrations, times devoted to service of those in need, and longer segments simply devoted to resting right when we need it most, that is, "in the bleak midwinter." Of course, some of your days will feature a mixture of some or all of these categories all at once, depending on how you choose to celebrate them.

One thing you will find conspicuously absent in this guide are many specific suggestions regarding gathered church worship. This is a deliberate absence. With the diversity of church backgrounds in mind, my assumption is people either attend congregations who already hold worship and prayer services throughout the 12 days (and thus already have prescribed liturgies) or people attend congregations who will more than likely never incorporate more times of worship and prayer into the 12 days anyway. Besides, if a congregation wants to start worshipping on the various feast days of the season, there are numerous denominational resources available to them, and thus you can sort out the details for yourself. The suggestions I do put forth in these pages hope to bridge the divide between those different kinds of worshipping communities. For example, whereas some churches may want to include some fun activities for children *after* their time of gathered worship and prayer on one of the feast days, other churches may want to have the same fun activities for that feast day and then encourage families to do prayer and devotions *at home*.

An underlying concern weaves its way throughout the entire book: how do we pass our traditions down to our children? Indeed, in many ways children are the primary consideration behind nearly all our Christmas celebrations, and they are a key emphasis in many of the suggestions in this book. Even so, in the midst of this concern lies a beautiful truth: the things we want for our children are the same things we want for ourselves. We want our children to truly know Christ and be able to worship him with all of their being. We want them to know the Story and to be able to tell that story to others. We want them to know how to selflessly give themselves to others and to have eyes to see when there are people in need around them. And we want them to carry this set of fun and meaningful traditions on into the future. More than likely, we are concerned our children will not learn these principles and rituals because we are bad at learning them ourselves. My hope is that this book can serve as a cross-generational guide where we can all be challenged to worship, celebrate, and serve during the 12 days of Christmas together.

There is another beautiful truth worth mentioning, one that is at the heart of this book. Initially we might approach the traditions of Christmas as a vast well of wisdom from which to draw, but eventually we come to realize that rather than merely preserving Christmas, we are instead being called to reinvent it altogether. By looking back at the past it becomes apparent that there are numerous traditions worth reviving, but that all of them will have to be adapted to the cultural contexts of the modern world. Looking at Christmas traditions over the span of history soon becomes overwhelming because there are too many practices and variations on those practices to choose from. It is difficult to be faithful to a tradition when there are in fact a vast number of traditions in the world. This is why, as much as this book is about me laying out the Christmas practices available before us, it is just as much about you considering and discerning what will work in your community. The liberating message of this book is that while we strive for faithfulness to our traditions, we are nonetheless free to adapt them into new forms and even invent some traditions of our own. Combining the new with the old just might be the most "in the spirit of Christmas" tradition we can participate in.

1

Misconceptions and Frequently Asked Questions about Christmas

AN INITIAL WARNING: DO NOT PUT THIS BOOK INTO PRACTICE BY YOURSELF!

WE LIVE IN A highly individualistic society. In some ways the needs and desires of the individual are valued above all else. Americans, in their *Declaration of Independence*, proclaim "life, liberty, and the pursuit of happiness" as their highest ideals, and in the ensuing centuries those ideals have tended to be given an increasingly individualistic interpretation: "*my* life, *my* liberty, *my* happiness."

But this humble book about Christmas has been written for the community, for the body of Christ, in all the various ways it takes form. Therefore I must start out with a warning: this book and its subject matter are not simply about *you*. Instead, it is about *us*, about how we as a group of people might celebrate the coming of Christ and fall down before him in worship *together*. My basic assumption is that you the individual will figure out how to make some of the ideas in these pages come alive in the living community that is Christ's body, the church.

Although I am an author, I am also a musician and church music leader, and one of the greatest joys in my life is getting a group of people to sing a song together. There is something awe-inspiring and joyous when a melody comes alive in someone's mind and heart, where a song inhabits a person and becomes part of them, even reshaping them a little. My prayer is the same for this book: that its thoughts and ideas become a melody that you sing everywhere and that in turn it even starts to sing *you*.

The basic question I want you to continually ask yourself as you read is, "I wonder how I can make this work in *my* community?" I can imagine receiving some immediate pushback with this suggestion because your "community" might take on any number of different forms. For the sake of establishing context, here are a few social groups this book was written for:

- The smallest and most obvious group is *your own family*. If you do not go to a church with a massive children's program or you are not yourself a children's or youth pastor, most everything suggested in this book can be scaled down and done within the realm of your own family. I think it is worth adding, though, that as you get acquainted with the suggested celebrations, you might want to think about inviting other families along or organizing a few of the events with a church small group. In some senses, the more people there are, the merrier, and you can always find more tasks for people to do as your group grows.

- The next and most obvious group is the *church congregation*. Whether your church has a large, efficient, and highly resourced children's program or you have a set of volunteer leaders for a small group of kids, the celebrations outlined in this book can be adapted to your context. Essentially, all you need are a group of kids who love to play, pretend, and make things, and a passionate, loving set of adults to lead them. Also, it should be noted that Christmas is a great time of the year to involve those in your church community who may not have children of their own or a family to spend time with. Getting them to enter in and help with your Christmas celebrations is truly a way to encourage the entire body of Christ to act together as one.

- Finally, these ideas could certainly work in the context of a *school or homeschool co-op*. Though Christian schools and homeschool groups are not the church itself but instead an extension of it, educational groups may want to consider ways to offer Christmas break activities for children in their area to attend. Not only would it be a service to parents during the mid-winter break, it would also be a unique way to attract people in your community to your school.

In chapter 4, as we begin to map out what we might want the 12 days to look like for us, I break these social groups down into further subgroups, but for now it is helpful to understand our traditions as operating within two primary categories: families, which are limited in number and thus more intimate, and community groups like churches, schools, and other civic organizations, which are essentially a gathered group from the general public.

To conclude: as you read through this book, let your imagination wander as you think of creative ways to celebrate the 12 days of Christmas with other people. Begin to see the entire season as a communal event where people come together to worship, to learn, to serve others, and to have a lot of fun.

So Are You Saying the Christmas Season Should Be Celebrated One Way?

In some ways, yes; in many ways, no. The first thing you will realize if you begin to research the history and traditions of Christmas, or if you converse with people from around the world about their own traditions, is there are entirely too many ways of celebrating it to choose from. The variations of traditions across time and culture are astounding. I specifically chose not to include every practice I came across, but to instead offer you three potential options. First, I specially curated what celebrations I believe make the most sense, both within the context of church history but also within modern societies, which meant not including some time-honored traditions of old. In other instances my suggestions combine traditions that are similar enough that they fit into the same general category as each other. Finally, I made a point to suggest innovative new ways to celebrate older traditions. This means that if your family, ethnic heritage, or church tradition celebrates Christmas in a way not outlined in this book, you are very much still welcome to celebrate in that way! What I include in the following chapters are my hearty suggestions compiled and curated from a wide swath of resources and traditions. And so, there really is no *one* way to celebrate Christmas.

And yet, at the same time, *all* Christmas practices fall into either one of four different categories:

- Worship
- Festive celebrating
- Service
- Rest

In actuality, you may say all festive seasonal traditions, both sacred and secular, follow this pattern. Sometimes all four categories can be found overlapping in a single event or sometimes only some of them are used, and yet they all naturally embed themselves into our communal celebrations. For instance, a typical American Independence Day might feature a solemn civic ceremony at a courthouse (worship), a fundraising event designed to help veterans (service), a backyard barbecue with lawn games that ends in attending a fireworks display (celebrating), as well as some much-needed downtime with family and friends (rest). Our Christmas season should follow a similar pattern, and, I would argue, it often already does. We attend Christmas worship with our congregation, we do a lot of fun celebrating, many of us engage in serving the needs of our community, and I would think that nearly all of us find time to slow down and get extra rest. In fact, these patterns are part of the normal rhythms of our lives in which we must be constantly seeking balance. One church ministry group has labeled the above categories as "UP, IN, OUT," and "Abiding."[1] "UP" is about how we relate to God, "IN" about how we relate to each other in the church, "OUT" about how we relate to the world around us, and "Abiding" about sabbathing in God in order that we may again go out and be productive. Finding balance in the rhythms of UP/IN/OUT/Abiding is how we become

---

1. Appleton, "Mid Sized Mission," 3 (based on the work of www.3dmovements.com).

a fruitful disciple of Jesus, and all four are embedded into the practices of Christmas.

While nearly all of us attend gathered worship at some point during the season, we most likely do not follow the full liturgical rhythm of the 12 days. Indeed, doing so may prove difficult for most contemporary Christians not already immersed in a church culture that celebrates the various holy days of the 12 days, but one of the primary aims of this book is to help us consider what new liturgical practices we may begin to incorporate into our communal, familial, and devotional lives. In the same way, I assume many of us know how to do "festive celebrating," at least when it comes to the conventionally modern tradition of gathering together to open presents, eat a large meal, and lie around the house the rest of the day. But might there be other, more diverse ways of celebrating that are simultaneously more communally engaging *and* more restful? My hope is to offer you a number of options that your family will want to make into long-lasting, meaningful, and fun traditions. Finally, even though we typically associate the Christmas season with giving to others and providing for those in need within our communities, how many of us actually go beyond giving a few canned items for a food drive that Other People are organizing in another section of town? My hope, though it is a challenging one, is to offer suggestions for how to truly see and then serve people's needs in our communities, as well as how we might go beyond merely surface-level and seasonal charity to seek more long-term societal solutions. Wherever we might find the most challenge within these pages, the main premise of this book is that the Christmas season must be a single, interconnected movement between worship, celebration, service, and rest. The only way Christmas will remain meaningful is if these four categories become inherently intertwined with our joyful and normal ways of celebrating.[2]

To conclude, while there might be one grand way to celebrate the holiday, there are nearly endless variations for how it can be planned out.

ARE THERE REALLY "12 DAYS OF CHRISTMAS"?

Yes, there are. First mentioned by the fourth-century theologian and hymn writer Ephrem the Syrian and made official in 567 at the Council of Tours,[3]

---

2. This complex understanding of what makes a culture great is the foundational argument of Joseph Pieper's *Leisure: the Basis of Culture*.

3. Miles, *Christmas Customs and Traditions*, 239.

Christmas is a 12-day season beginning at sundown on Christmas Eve (December 24), extending until January 5, and culminating in the Feast of the Epiphany (the visiting of the Magi) on January 6. However, depending on how we determine when days begin and end, this time span actually includes *more* than 12 days. Historically, there have been a number of conceptions for when the 12 days occur, which might make the practice of celebrating it confusing for some. For instance, it could be 12 days from December 25 to January 5, 12 days and an evening if you count the 24th (according to the older conception of days beginning at sundown), or 13 days if you count Epiphany as part of the larger season. There is one conception of the season that views the 24th as the first night of Christmas, a shift which would then make Twelfth Night occur on January 4, and there is still another tradition that claims the "first day" of Christmas is December 26, the day *after* Christmas Day. Viewed this way, Twelfth Night would occur on January 6, the Feast of the Epiphany.[4] As much as it would be wonderful for Christmas to bookend right into Epiphany, calling December 26 the first day of Christmas causes immediate numerical and cultural head-scratching and thus it is not worth changing it to the "first night" in my opinion. Regarding Christmas Eve, I believe it is best to continue calling it the eve of Christmas (even though it is the official start of Christmas) and the evening of December 25 the first night of Christmas. In this conception of the season Christmas ends at "Twelfth Night" on January 5 and Epiphany (both as a feast day and a loosely held season) begins on January 6.

In light of this potential confusion I believe it is important to emphasize something right from the start: instead of getting hung up on the exact number days of Christmas, we should instead approach the days as one continuous movement, much like we do from Palm Sunday to Holy Week to Easter, of which—to my knowledge—no one counts the exact number of days, even though the number of days are in fact predetermined. In Easter we are drawn into the progression from Christ's Triumphal Entry to the Last Supper to Gethsemane to his trial, death, resurrection, and ascension. Likewise, the progression of Advent through Christmas takes us through numerous events surrounding the coming of Christ: there are the prophecies foretelling his birth, the preparation of John the Baptist's ministry, the annunciation of Christ's birth (along with Mary's and Joseph's reactions), his birth in Bethlehem, the coming of the Magi to Herod (and his slaying of the innocents), Jesus's circumcision and naming, the visit of the Magi to

---

4. Miles, *Christmas Customs and Traditions*, 239.

the Holy Family, and his presentation in the temple. There really are a lot of episodes in the story, and making Christmas into a season (with Advent as its precursor) allows us to give each part its proper due. In this way the Advent and Christmas season becomes first a four-Sunday period of drawing back in preparation for Christ's coming and then a 12-day (or so) midwinter festival where everyone slows down and we spend lots of time with our family and the broader community celebrating the coming of Christ.

However, it is worth noting that historically the Christmas season as a whole has been configured in different ways as well. For instance, there is the Christmas octave, which is the first eight days of Christmas from December 25 to January 1, shortening the season to a proper week. It has also been configured as a forty-day season ending on February 2 with Candlemas or the Feast of the Presentation of Our Lord, when Jesus was presented in the temple after Mary's days of purification were completed.[5] In the forty-day conception of Christmas (often called Christmastide), the season extends into a season of ordinary time; but in some church traditions is coming to be viewed as the *season* of Epiphany, where the Gospel readings recount the various "epiphanies" of Christ before and during his public ministry: Christ's baptism, his first miracle at the wedding in Cana, and all the way to Transfiguration Sunday right before Lent begins. Although not officially recognized on the church calendar, the combined season of Advent, Christmas, and Epiphany can be viewed as one long meditation of preparation and response to Christ's first appearing and all his subsequent appearances or "epiphanies" throughout the Gospels.

Another conception of the Christmas season, to the great irritation of church calendar purists, is how American culture has essentially shifted Christmas from the day after Thanksgiving (the fourth Thursday of November) until December 25, with Christmas being considered over with on the 26th. In some ways we unofficially keep an extended Christmas season from the 25th until New Year's Day, although for the most part American culture celebrates Christmas and New Year's as two completely separate holidays only related by their proximity on the calendar. It should be noted, however, that in some countries the beginning of Christmas coincides with Advent, as with St. Lucia's Day on December 13 in Nordic countries, St. Nicholas's Day on December 6 in Czechia, the Feast of the Immaculate Conception on December 8 in Germanic countries (being what is called a

---

5. Filz, "Does Christmas End on Epiphany?" para. 5.

novena), or the eight days leading up to December 25 in Italy.[6] Despite its cultural prominence in the United States, this non-church-calendar-related tendency to bleed Christmas backwards into the season of Advent must be resisted (for reasons that will be made evident later in this chapter as well as in the chapter on Advent), and we must instead devote ourselves to developing robust and compelling holiday practices for Advent, Christmas, and Epiphany in hopes of eventually shifting our cultures back to a 12-day conception of Christmas beginning on the evening of December 24.

One final confusion about the season must be addressed: none of the major traditions within the church agrees on a single Christmas calendar. Fortunately, Roman Catholics, the Orthodox Church, and various Protestant traditions follow the same 12 days from December 24 and 25 to January 5, however the specific feast days in each tradition vary from each other. For example, within Anglicanism January 1, being the eighth day of Christmas, is the Feast of the Holy Name or Feast of the Circumcision, whereas in Catholicism it is the Solemnity of Mary, the Mother of God (the Roman Church changed the day back to its presumed older designation as a feast to Mary during the Second Vatican Council). There are also a number of minor feast days specific to each tradition, such as—to name only a few—St. Thomas Becket (Catholic and Anglican), John Wyclif (Anglican), St. Sylvester (Catholic), and the twenty thousand martyrs burned in Nicomedia (Orthodox). A more significant difference occurs between the Eastern and Western churches on Epiphany, where the Eastern Orthodox celebrate Christ's baptism on January 6, whereas Western churches celebrate the visitation of the Wise Men on that date.[7]

All the variations between the traditions aside, I believe there is a way for the worldwide church to unite around the posture of worship and celebration inherent to the 12 of days Christmas. In hopes of attempting some semblance of Church unity, it is important to reclaim Christmas as a shared season where we all gather together to contemplate the mystery of God come to earth to save humanity in the time from Christmas Eve, to the twelfth night on January 5, to the Feast of the Epiphany on January 6.

---

6. Baker, *Discovering Christmas Customs*, 7.

7. To look at the various church calendars side-by-side a simple internet search will bring up the primary websites for each tradition. Search for "Roman Catholic calendar," "Eastern Orthodox calendar," or whatever specific tradition or denomination you need.

SO. . .WHAT'S THE "12 DAYS OF CHRISTMAS" SONG ABOUT THEN?

In some ways, the playfully ridiculous carol "The 12 Days of Christmas" is the whole reason this book is being written. Growing up, the song was always an unexplainable absurdity to me, something whose meaning never made sense for two reasons. First, I had no idea how all the gifts of the 12 days related to each other or to Christmas, and I did not understand why those 12 items would be chosen as gifts in the first place (For instance, does anyone need that many birds? And in what kind of world do people give leaping lords and milking maids as gifts to their loved one?). Second, I did not know what the 12 days of Christmas were, as no one I knew actually celebrated the season in that way. In complete ignorance I began to imagine a scenario where first each of the 12 days of Christmas had its own individual title and history, and then that there was a certain tradition attached to each of the gifts in the song, which increased in both proportion and absurdity throughout the season.

Here are the basics regarding the song's origins. First, it is significant to note it was a "forfeit game" song that was sung as a Twelfth Night celebration, which I will explain about below. Next, it was most likely originally a French carol, but it was first published in English in 1780 and has been published with *many* variations in the lyrics since that time (most especially in what the gifts of each day are). Finally, it was combined with its most well-known melody in 1909 by English composer Frederick Austin (who used a traditional tune).[8]

To me, the most liberating aspect of learning the song's history is that it was written in the form of a silly parlor song known as a forfeit game and was often sung for fun on Twelfth Night by both adults and children, as described by Alice Bertha Gomme in 1894:

> The leader of the game commenced by saying the first line. . .The lines for the "first day" of Christmas was said by each of the company in turn; then the first "day" was repeated, with the addition of the "second" by the leader, and then this was said all round the circle in turn. This was continued until the lines for the "twelve days" were said by every player. For every mistake a forfeit—a small article belonging to the person—had to be given up. These forfeits were afterwards "cried" in the usual way, and were not

---

8. Lawson-Jones, *Why was the Partridge in the Pear Tree?*, 58–68.

returned to the owner until they had been redeemed by the penalty inflicted being performed.[9]

Thus the main idea of a forfeit game was to sing each verse of the song with increasing speed in hopes of catching someone out, forcing them to drop out of the game, with the winner being "the one who could remember all the items in order, being able to recite at speed."[10] In this way, "The 12 Days of Christmas" is similar to my friends and I singing "Ninety-nine Bottles of Beer on the Wall" or "This is the Song That Doesn't End" as acts of endurance coming home from long school bus trips as kids. The difference with a forfeit game though is there were consequences, much like (if you will forgive the reference) the modern equivalent of strip poker (but for kids!). What has been liberating about this realization is that it has helped me move past attempting to find a deeper meaning or connection between all the gifts and how they relate to Christmas. It is simply a fun song for us to sing, though looking at the historical record might be a good motivation to reinstitute the forfeit game elements into our singing of it, perhaps even on Twelfth Night itself.

Nonetheless, an unfortunate legend surrounding the song has continued to persist, supposedly originating with a Catholic priest in the 1990s, which was that it was intended to be used as a secret catechizing tool by Catholics during eras of persecution in England (roughly the sixteenth to nineteenth centuries).[11] The idea of the legend is that Catholic teachings were hidden inside the verses of the song, with each of the successive gifts representing aspects of the faith needing to be kept hidden for fear of being exposed.[12] There are two simple problems with this theory. First, the historical record gives no indication that the song was written or sung for this use during this time period, and second (perhaps even more significantly), the recommended symbols ascribed to each verse were still very much in line with the Church of England's own core doctrines. In other words, there

---

9. Gomme, *The Traditional Games of England, Scotland, and Ireland*, 319.

10. Lawson-Jones, *Why was the Partridge in the Pear Tree?* 62.

11. Stockert, "The Twelve Days of Christmas." A more thorough investigation into the potential origins of the secret Catholic catechism theory can be found at Mikkelson, "The Twelve Days of Christmas."

12. This is the assertion found in many general-audience books and articles, such as in writer Ace Collins's *Stories behind the Best-loved Songs of Christmas*, 169–75; Collins offers no citations and conjures out of thin air a false history regarding the song's relation to Catholic persecution.

would have been no need to encrypt secret meanings in this fashion. To demonstrate, the days are often designated this way:

Day 1	Jesus, our savior
Day 2	The Old and New Testaments
Day 3	The Trinity, the three gifts of the Magi, or the virtues of faith, hope, and love
Day 4	The four Gospels
Day 5	The Pentateuch
Day 6	The six days of creation
Day 7	The seven gifts of the Holy Spirit
Day 8	The eight beatitudes
Day 9	The nine fruits of the Holy Spirit
Day 10	The Ten Commandments
Day 11	The eleven faithful apostles
Day 12	The twelve tribes of Israel or the twelve tenets of the Apostles' Creed

Although using the song as a catechetical tool has the potential to be confusing to people, as any relation between the gifts and aspects of the Christian faith are arbitrary and ascribed after the fact, some communities may still want to find creative ways of doing so, just as long as the Catholic Conspiracy Theory (as I call it) ceases to be attached to it.

Getting back to its known history, the song is thought to be French in origin for two reasons. First, partridges were not known to perch in pear trees in England until the red-legged French partridge was introduced to the island in the 1770s (long after the game had become popular), and second, "pear tree" sounds notably close to "perdrix," the French word for "partridge."[13] These French origins show how the lyrics were adapted into new forms over successive generations as they were translated into English. Though first published in English in 1780 in the book *Mirth Without Mischief*,[14] the lyrics had been sung or recited since perhaps the early eighteenth century[15] with various alterations over the years. As merely one example, instead of "A partridge in a pear tree," some of the other variations are "a partridge *on* a pear tree," "part of a juniper tree," or "a partridge up a pear tree."[16] There has also been speculation as to whether or not the first seven gifts were all references to birds and the "five golden rings" originally referred to the rings on a pheasant's neck (or some other kind of bird),[17] though it should be noted that in the 1780 publication of *Mirth without Mischief*, five actual gold rings are depicted in the drawn illustration accompanying those lyrics. One final significant lyrical change worth mentioning is the lyric "four calling birds" as we know it today used to be "collie birds," an archaic name for blackbirds, in the 1780 version. When the more modern version was solidified in 1909 people simply did not know what "collie birds" referred to, and thus it was changed.[18]

Finally, for the sake of fun it is worth mentioning that the song offers a clever numerical gimmick. It is not clear how intentional this was in its composition, but when all the gifts given out are added up together, their sum is 364, enough to last us until *next* Christmas. That is:

$$1 + 3 + 6 + 10 + 15 + 21 + 28 + 36 + 45 + 55 + 66 + 78 = 364$$

---

13. Lawson-Jones, *Why Was the Partridge in the Pear Tree?* 63.

14. *Mirth without Mischief*, 5–16.

15. Husk, *Songs of the Nativity*, 181. Writing in 1864, of the song Husk said, "This piece is found on broadsides printed at Newcastle at various periods during the last hundred and fifty years."

16. Sharp et al, "Forfeit Songs," 279.

17. Baring-Gould and Baring-Gould, *The Annotated Mother Goose*, 197.

18. Austin, "The Twelve Days of Christmas."

But You Don't Really Believe Jesus Was Born on December 25, Do You? And Wasn't the Date Just Chosen By the Church to Replace More Popular Pagan Holidays of the Time?

Multiple volumes and scores of scholarly articles have been and continue to be written in an attempt to answer the question of why we celebrate Christmas on December 25.[19] Frustratingly, the historical record continues to remain too vague for researchers to give us a definite answer, but the debate for the origins of Christmas comes down to two major and two minor theories.

The first major theory is the *History of Religions Theory*, which posits that the date of Christmas was established by the early church as a reaction to the pagan Roman practices of the day, though scholars debate whether that reaction was direct and intentional, or if the culture of the day had a "soft" influence, "conscious or unconscious," on the church.[20] Most notable is a feast for the sun deity Sol, known as the "unconquered sun" (the feast is often called *Dies Natalis Solis Invicti*, or Sol Invictus for short reference), which is noted as occurring on December 25, according to an ancient Roman timeline called the *Chronograph of 354*.[21] In another section of the *Chronograph* it also mentions, at the beginning of a list of Christian martyrs, that Christ was born on December 25. Though its title proclaims it was written in 354 CE, there is an indication it was originally compiled in 336 CE, and thus the earliest undisputed evidence for December 25 as the agreed date of Christmas, though specifically in Rome, comes from the early- to mid-fourth century.

The 25th was originally the date of the winter solstice (which was officially changed to the actual solstice date of December 21 at the Council of Nicaea in 325); because of the old solstice date, Emperor Aurelian inaugurated the feast of Sol Invictus in 274 to commemorate the "rebirth" of the sun on the darkest night of the year, as the days began to once again

---

19. The amount of scholarship on the subject is vast and reading through it all can be daunting. The information laid out in this section was culled from the following sources, with more specific information being footnoted separately: Roll, *Toward the Origins of Christmas;* Miles, *Christmas Customs and Traditions,* 165–71; Connell, *On God and Time;* Bradshaw and Johnson, *The Origins of Feasts;* Talley, *The Origins of the Liturgical Year;* Kelly, *The Origins of Christmas;* Gunstone, *Christmas and Epiphany.*

20. Roll, private email correspondence, May 2019.

21. Schmidt, "Calculating December 25," 542–43.

lengthen. Christmas is also often mistakenly associated with two other pagan festivals, namely Saturnalia (December 17–23) and the Kalends (January 1–5)—which was the Roman New Year—despite the fact that neither of their dates actually correspond with Christmas Day (though they do fall in the general category of "midwinter festival"). Whatever the associated festival, the History of Religions Theory asserts that the early church instituted Christmas on December 25 to combat or replace the bacchanalian, idol worshipping practices of Rome. In many ways, this theory has been and continues to be the most widely believed in the broader culture, as well as among church historians.

Even so, there is no direct proof that the church started celebrating the birth of Christ or that they specifically chose December 25 to combat pagan practices. In fact, many of the church's early pastors and theologians sought to distance themselves from any practices that resembled the Roman or more regional expressions of pagan worship and celebration. On top of this, there simply is not any great proof that Sol Invictus was a prominent Roman holiday. Being instituted in only 274 meant that it hardly had any time to establish itself as a popular tradition before the Christian era of Emperor Constantine. Besides that, the sun was never a prominent Roman deity but instead a ubiquitous symbol in the Roman world (often paired with Luna the moon) which was depicted in a variety of mediums (almost like we use trademarked brand names today) and was given other, more prominent feast days on the Roman calendar.[22] In other words, as according to scholar Steven Hijmans, Christmas on December 25 was not established to compete with Sol Invictus because the holiday was simply not prominent enough, and the sun as a concept "played an ambiguous role in the Roman world both as a cosmic body and as a god."[23]

The second major theory, called *The Calculation Theory*, posits "that the December 25th birth of Christ was calculated from the annunciation and conception [March 25], which in turn was obtained from the supposed date of Christ's passion."[24] Related to this calculation is the early church's belief that Jesus also died on March 25, coinciding with the Passover.[25] Also

22. Hijmans, "Sol Invictus." These are the primary arguments Hijmans makes throughout this article, which seriously calls into question the legitimacy of the History of Religions Theory.

23. Hijmans, "Sol Invictus," 395.

24. Simmons, "The Origins of Christmas," 303.

25. Nothaft, "Early Christian Chronology," 249, 260.

related to this date is the birth of John the Baptist, who according to Luke 1:26 was conceived six months before Jesus and has his feast day on June 24, which is indeed six months before Christmas.

But is it even probable to work from calculations (and speculations) surrounding Jesus's birth as a means of determining a remotely accurate date? To start with, some scholars have attempted to calculate when John's father Zechariah might have been serving in the temple as a priest in the "division of Abijah" (Luke 1:5), concluding, according to a complicated amount of discernment between the priestly cycles and the Israelite lunar calendars, that "the nativity probably took place either between late June and very early August, or between mid January and fairly early February. A date in the depths of winter is therefore one of the two possibilities."[26] Another area of contention that relates to the calculations debate is when the census would most likely have been taken, with scholars possibly favoring an August–October date, as that falls between harvest time and the wet season, whereas a winter date during the wet season would have made travel difficult for people.[27] And still another area of discrepancy relates to the shepherds, where there are conflicting accounts about whether or not it was realistic for them to have been out in the fields in midwinter, with some sources claiming the conditions of Palestine are ideal for grazing at that time of the year and that the shepherds would not have been in the wilderness but close to Bethlehem as the sheep could have been used for temple sacrifices, and other sources claiming Palestine's conditions would have been too harsh, with the potential for deep snow at that time of the year.[28] Unfortunately, I was not able to locate any actual studies done on the patterns of first-century Israelite shepherds in general or the Bethlehem shepherds in particular. One fascinating study by Kurt M. Simmons that relates to the Calculation Theory is how the coinciding timelines of Herod's death before Passover (which is relatively agreed upon by historians), the visitation of the Magi first with Herod and then with the Holy Family several months after Christ's birth, a recorded lunar eclipse, and the slaying of the innocents in Bethlehem all support the claim that "the traditional date of Christ's birth is historically defensible and sound."[29] As astonishing as

26. Beckwith, "St. Luke," 94.

27. Beckwith, "St. Luke," 76–77.

28. For these conflicting reports see Gibson, "The Date of Christ's Birth," para. 3–10, and Deems, *Holy Days and Holidays*, 405.

29. Simmons, "The Origins of Christmas," 310–20, quote from 310.

this theory is, I unfortunately have yet to find any other scholars responding to or verifying the theory Simmons has put forward.

It is worth noting how the cosmological symbolism embedded in the December 25 date coincides with the winter solstice, which would have been appealing to the early church as a sign showing God's sovereign aligning of the cosmos with that of salvation history. Christ, who is the true Son of Righteousness, was born at the solstice or "rebirth" of the sun. John the Baptist, however, would have been conceived on the autumnal equinox and born at the summer solstice, "which marks the beginning of decreasing day-length" and corresponds symbolically to John's assertion in John 3:30 that "he [Jesus] must increase, but I must decrease."[30] Along with this, many in the early church believed the world was created on March 25, and thus the vernal or spring equinox, in which Christ was believed to be conceived and to die, corresponds to major cosmic events.[31] Please do not interpret this wrongly: this was not the early church bending over backward to make Jesus's life fit into a pagan conception of the world; instead this was their way of being scientific and historically precise to the best of their abilities, in an attempt to reason out what they thought they knew of the cosmos and the life of Christ. Whether or not Jesus actually *was* born on December 25, the establishment of the date represents a growing consensus (for their time) of how God's plan of salvation through the sending of his Son related to the ordering of the universe. To them, this was a clear way in which the heavens very literally were declaring the glory of God (Psalm 19:1).

There were certainly disputes about the date for Christ's birth, most notably in how January 6 was almost certainly the date accepted earlier in the church's history, at least by the Eastern churches. Martin Connell, in looking at the worshipping community of Ambrose, bishop of Milan (c. 340–397), assesses how January 6 was somewhat widely accepted as a date for Christ's birth, while obviously still in a state of development:

> Unlike Christmas, about which we are not sure, Epiphany *was* being celebrated in Milan during Ambrose's episcopate; further, Epiphany had earlier included the "birthday of the Savior" in its narrative embrace in churches in the East and in at least a few churches in the West. Moreover, the non-nativity scriptural references included by Ambrose in the recollection—the wedding feast

30. Nothaft, "Early Christian Chronology," 260.
31. Schmidt, "Calculating December 25," 542, 545, 548.

of Cana and the multiplication miracle—are elsewhere ascribed to Epiphany in Milan at the time of Ambrose's writing.[32]

Connell asserts it is possible that, in Ambrose's day, both the nativity and the visitation of the Magi were celebrated on the same date, January 6, as a series of manifestations (that is, epiphanies) of Christ.[33] Eastern Orthodox churches still celebrate Christ's baptism on January 6 rather than the coming of the Magi, calling it the Feast of the Theophany, with some churches still celebrating the nativity on that date as well (such as in Armenia), with the most likely reason being that Luke 3:23 notes how Jesus was "about thirty years of age" when he was baptized and began his public ministry, thus correlating the time of his baptism with his birthday. But why January 6, rather than December 25, or any other date in the year, for that matter? The answer to this question leads us to consider the first minor theory mentioned at the beginning of this section, which I do not believe has a formal title so I will choose to call it the *Church Fathers Tradition Theory*, which simply states that December 25 (or January 6) was the date handed down through the oral tradition of the early church.[34] This is a difficult theory to swallow as it's not entirely verifiable (and many scholars do not take it seriously), though there are a number of tangential and explicit references to December 25 and Christ's birth in a significant number of works from the second to the fourth centuries, including Hippolytus's *Canon* and *Chronicon*, Julius Africanus's *Chronographie*, Clement of Alexandria's *Stromata*, the *Pascha Computus*, the Gnostic offshoot group known as the Basilidians, Pope Telesphorus's *Liber Pontificalis*, Egeria's account of her pilgrimage to Jerusalem, the poems and writings of Ephrem the Syrian, and some sermons by Augustine, John Chrysostom, and Ambrose. Each of these writings contains a reference to December 25 as a possible date for the birth, and Augustine even went so far as to claim that Christ himself chose December 25 due to the cosmic symbolism mentioned above, which is pure conjecture (about the Son of God!), but examples like this can show how the Church Fathers at least thought the date may have been handed down authentically.[35] The problem with all of these sources is that consensus on the date only begins to truly form, beginning in the Western church, in the

32. Connell, "Did Ambrose's Sister," 147.

33. Connell, "Did Ambrose's Sister," 150.

34. Simmons, "The Origins of Christmas," 302; and Marshall, "Yes, Christ Was Really Born on December 25."

35. Roll, *Toward the Origins of Christmas*, 103.

late fourth century, and thus there are no direct sources showing that the date was handed down from the Apostles or other church leaders in the early era. This leads us to the final minor theory.

Förster's Theory, posited by papyrologist Hans Förster, "essentially holds that Christmas emerged as the result of fourth-century Holy Land Tourism. As pilgrims flocked to Bethlehem to visit the original site of the nativity, they began to celebrate a corresponding annual festival in mid-winter, which they eventually exported back to their home communities."[36] There is certainly historical weight to Förster's Theory, but most scholars see it as too one-dimensional, not robust enough to address the complexities and vacancies of the historical record. In light of what we know, there seems to be a growing consensus to want to put all of the theories in conversation with each other, with the History of Religions Theory fading most into the background: "it is no longer helpful to view the introduction of Christmas as the one-sided reaction to a pre-existing pagan tradition. Much rather, they apparently were parallel phenomena, different outgrowth, so to speak, of the same *Zeitgeist*."[37]

I will conclude this section with two lengthy quotes from leading scholars in this field. Noting that Christians have always struggled with how to live within cultures antithetical to the faith, Susan K. Roll asserts, as noted above, it does not make sense that early Christians would have instituted the feast of Christ's Nativity as a "baptized pagan feast" since they had been struggling for so long to differentiate themselves from the Roman Empire. At the same time, being able to practice their faith more unhindered amidst a "post Constantinian freedom," the rituals of the faith certainly started to look more like the ceremonies of imperial Rome. Christmas emerges right in the middle of this cultural shift and it is here

> where the waters get really murky as far as how you evaluate levels of probability as far as the origin, time period, and driving motivation for instituting a feast of Christ's Nativity, keeping in mind that this was all local in nature to Rome and North Africa as of 360 or so (they had it, the East didn't) . . . [About what it comes down to is] what kind of conjecture is defensible conjecture? . . . Where can you stop and say "we have no hard proof but this is a likely scenario based on what we have"? What scholars have to do is evaluate the relative probability based on the materials they have

36. Nothaft, "Early Christian Chronology," 250.
37. Nothaft, "The Origins of the Christmas Date," 909.

and the best evaluation they can do of that material *in situ*, in its own context, to the best of our knowledge.[38]

Historian Philipp Nothaft offers a similar assessment that is initially unsatisfying in its inconclusiveness but sobering in its attempt to consider the full scope of the historical record in the search for the origins of the date for Christmas:

> It will no longer do to simply juxtapose HRT [History of Religions Theory] and CT [Calculuation Theory] as sharp alternatives. Indeed, one of the most encouraging trends in recent research on Christmas's history is its critical stance towards sweeping narratives and a readiness to consider explanations that are more multifaceted and to accept a more diverse range of factors than has previously been the case. Whether we will eventually be treated to a definitive account on this basis, ultimately depends on the ability of future scholars to order the existing tangle of terse and often conflicting sources in new and creative ways.[39]

WHAT DO I TELL MY KIDS ABOUT SANTA CLAUS?

Whether you have children, plan to have children, or there are children in your life, I believe it is best to begin handling "the Santa Claus issue" by asking yourself two initial questions: who *is* Santa Claus (or Saint Nicholas), and who is Santa Claus to *you*? Although I am writing a book about Christmas, and have thus presumptively set myself up as an authority on the holiday, I will nonetheless ultimately defer to a general "Christian freedom" when it comes to making my recommendations about this subject. However, regarding the first question, I believe it is worth it to consider separating "Santa Claus" from Nicholas of Myra, a fourth-century bishop from present-day southern Turkey and a saint of the church whose feast day is December 6. "Santa Claus," as he is rendered in the popular imagination, is most certainly a mythological character akin to a pagan god, with hardly any remaining connection to the real-life saint. First, let us consider St. Nick, the real person.

---

38. Roll, unpublished interview. Roll makes similar points but with more information in her section "Some Historical Perspectives," in Slee and Miles's *Doing December Differently*, 118–20.

39. Nothaft, "The Origins of the Christmas Date," 910–11.

While the veracity of many of the stories told about Saint Nicholas is in question, four of the most well-known relate to Christmas (at least tangentially).[40] In the first, and most retold, Nicholas was said to have heard of an impoverished father in his town who had three daughters but no dowries to provide for their marriages; they were therefore faced with the possibility of being forced into prostitution. For three consecutive nights, one for each of the daughters, Nicholas took a bag of gold and left it on the windowsill of their home. As the entry point for St. Nick's penchant for gift giving, an addendum to this story is how the benevolent bishop came to be known for leaving gold in the shoes of those who left them out for him on the eve of his feast day, hence the tradition of leaving out our stockings to be filled, traditionally with oranges or gold chocolate coins.

The second story, a seeming mixture of fact and fiction, is that Nicholas, while attending the Council of Nicaea (potentially fact), got angry at the Arian heretics (or Arius himself!), and ended up slapping (or in some accounts punching) one of them (this, almost certainly a fiction). Though a humorous legend, this anecdote is noteworthy for how it links Nicholas to the doctrine established at Nicaea that is integral to Christ's incarnation (and thus Christmas) in that Jesus is the Son of God eternally begotten from, and of the same substance as, the Father, and not the created son of God who came into existence at a point in time, as the Arians believed.

The third story is a legend that he once rebuked and calmed a storm at sea while on voyage to the Holy Land, which eventually resulted in him being given the title patron saint of sailors. Claiming him as their own, sailors and ex-sailors began buying presents for their families on Nicholas's Day, giving the lesser gifts on December 6 and reserving the better presents for Christmas itself.[41] Finally, in a morbid story from which Nicholas came to be associated as the patron saint of children (and Christmas is all but our most child-centric holiday) he is said to have rescued and resurrected three dead children who had been pickled in a barrel for food during a famine by an evil butcher.[42]

As you may have noticed, apart from its proximity on the calendar, it's not immediately apparent how the saint and his feast day came to be

---

40. For various sources on Saint Nicholas and the development of Santa Claus mythology, see Bowler, *Encyclopedia of Christmas*, 155–6; McNight, *St. Nicholas*, 37–52; Hervey, *The Book of Christmas*; and www.stnicholascenter.org.

41. McKnight, *St. Nicholas*, 37–52.

42. Ferguson, *Signs and Symbols in Christian Art*, 135–36.

associated with the nativity of Christ. Here it becomes increasingly important for you to discern for yourself the answer to the second question above, that is, who Santa Claus is *for you*, for we must certainly begin distinguishing the man, Nicholas of Myra—whose own historical record is murky enough—from the various manifestations of the legendary character of Santa Claus, the Dutch Sinterklaas, the British Father Christmas, or whatever name and manifestation he happens to go by. Depending on your national heritage or which stories are most appealing to you, Santa Claus can range from being the rotund, gift-giving, reindeer-accompanied, jolly old elf from the North Pole that most Americans are used to; to the supernatural saint keeping track of every child's wrongdoing from the previous year (a belief also popular in America); to the more ambivalent (though still gift-giving) figure who shows up at our door paired with any one of a potential array of justice-wielding companions equipped with a birch or willow rod and ready to strike sinful children, such as Knecht Ruprecht, Black Pete, or the goat demon Krampus (though sometimes Santa himself comes ready to strike with the rod!).[43] Really, this is only the beginning, as the variations about Santa and myriad other gift-bringing mythological Christmas characters are nearly as many as the European countries from which they derive (I go into this subject more in chapter 3 on St. Nicholas and St. Lucia).

Here now, allow me to offer my own recommendations. To start with, I believe we should get back to celebrating St. Nicholas on his feast day, and dissociating him with Christmas Day itself. Doing so (and again, I discuss this more in the chapter about him) allows us to place Nicholas as a saint to model our lives after more broadly within the Advent and Christmas seasons so that we may focus more on the coming of Christ at Christmas. Next, we must ask ourselves whether or not we want to introduce the supernatural, the mythical, and the realm of make-believe into our children's Christmas tradition. In my own family, not wanting to lie to our children (and not being particularly good at it), we have chosen not to attempt to get our children to believe in Santa Claus or any Christmas-related legend, but neither do we speak about those practices as being evil. We have taught our children the most prominent story about St. Nicholas of Myra and in the years to come hope to institute some of the traditions associated with his day when December 5th and 6th come around again. Our children have also seen a number of films about Santa, which we approach like any other

43. Bowler, *Encyclopedia of Christmas*, 128, 257, 198–200.

fantasy film or story. I myself truly believed in Santa until I was about seven or eight and I did not resent my parents when I discovered the truth (nor did it damage my belief in God), but when it came to shaping my own children's experience of Christmas I simply did not have the conviction to continue this tradition, and instead wanted the supernatural aspect of the season to be the miracle of the Son of God becoming flesh. There is a part of me that laments that we have done this, but I believe there are an abundance other ways for fantasy, make-believe, and belief in the supernatural to become essential ingredients in my children's lives without convincing them a jolly elf is bringing them presents every year. Again, I ultimately leave the decision up to individual families, though I would challenge those who decide to continue the Santa tradition to truly discern *which* Santa or mythical Christmas tradition they want to practice, as our current practices are a relatively recent variation[44] and there really are too many Santa traditions to choose from if you look at the history. Further, I contend that there are significant problems with the Santa Claus myth for followers of Christ, as I discuss in the next section. You could, as became popular in post-Reformation Germanic countries, tell your children that the Christ Child himself, or the Christkindl, brings the presents on Christmas morning, though in my opinion that practice could *actually* be damaging to children in the long run!

ISN'T CHRISTMAS JUST A PAGAN HOLIDAY THOUGH?

When answering questions regarding the pagan origins of Christmas, it is so easy to immediately entrench ourselves in a black-and-white argument where the other side is so obviously wrong and our side is in the right. In recent years I have read a slew of articles stating the "obvious" truth about the origins of the various Christmas traditions that have been handed down to us, with one side pointing to the inarguable pagan roots of the holiday (or the general winter season) as handed down from a mixture of Mediterranean, Roman, and northern European traditions, and the other side pointing to the clearly pure intentions of the early church in creating a holiday for the growing devotion to Christ's nativity (and thus the *absence* of pagan origins for the holiday). Personally, as should be obvious, I am most certainly given to the latter kinds of arguments, but I believe it is important

---

44. McKibben, *Hundred Dollar Holiday*, 25–37. For a full account of the development of the American Santa Claus see Nissenbaum, *The Battle for Christmas*.

to live into the tensions and gray areas of our shared histories, rather than pretending they are not there in order that "our side" can win the ongoing cultural and historical debate. I think it is important to acknowledge from the start that history is complicated and layered, and our answers to tough questions about history should therefore reflect this complexity.

With this in mind, I will attempt to answer the pagan problem of Christmas in two seemingly contradictory parts, which I admit is intentionally provocative:

1. We should seek to either eliminate or transform all variations of paganism from our Christmas celebrations.

2. Due to the state of our modern world, it would benefit us to inject some good, old-fashioned paganism back into Christmas!

To the first point, I am of the opinion that the church should seek to eliminate (or transform!) paganism in whatever form it comes in, and this certainly applies to its practices surrounding Christmas. But what exactly is "paganism"? While the word can certainly be attached to a vast array of peoples and practices (ancient and modern), I am most interested in what we think we mean when we hear someone say, "That's pagan. Christians shouldn't do that." At the risk of formulating an inadequately short list, here is what I think most Christians can agree on regarding paganism:

1. It is the worship of false gods and idols instead of the one true God, or the worship of created nature instead of God, the creator of nature.

2. It assumes a posture of fear toward divinity, where people are forever needing to make sacrifices to appease the gods or atone for their sins. Out of this stems all manner of superstitious practices, where people perform some kind of ritual to manipulate the gods in order to effect a desired result or to avoid judgment from the gods.

3. It can often describe a hedonistic, indulgent, moral deviance, the opposite of the holiness God is calling us to.

Believe it or not, all three of those definitions of paganism have found their way into plenty of our well-accepted Christmas traditions. That is to say, if we look back at Christmas history we will find various Christian peoples worshipping false gods, practicing all kinds of fear-based superstitions, and giving in to all manner of sinful indulgences. Therefore, when it comes to a particular practice surrounding the holiday, we should simply ask ourselves if it is entering into any of those pagan descriptions, and, if so, we should stop (or walk away from) that particular practice, whether it occurs in the church, the community, or the family. All other practices not falling into those categories, I would argue, are open to Christian freedom. Our task is to always be discerning what a tradition is in itself signifying or performing through its being acted out, and not necessarily if it has "pagan" roots.

Let's take two traditions as examples: decorating with a Christmas tree, lights, and various greenery, and then telling children Santa knows if they have been "naughty or nice" throughout the year. Regarding the first example, decorating homes with lights and greenery has long been associated with pagan practices and the worship of idols and was criticized as early as the second or third century CE by Tertullian, who derisively wrote of Christians who engaged in the practice:

> "Then," do you say, "the lamps before my doors, and the laurels on my posts are an honour to God?" They are there of course, not because they are an honour to God, but to him who is honour [sic] in God's stead by ceremonial observances of that kind, so far as is manifest, saving the religious performance, which is in secret appertaining to demons. For we ought to be sure if there are any whose notice it escapes through ignorance of this world's literature, that there are among the Romans even gods of entrances; Cardea (Hinge-goddess), called after hinges, and Forculus (Door-god) after doors, and Limentius (Threshold-god) after the threshold, and Janus himself (Gate-god) after the gate: and of course we know that, though names be empty and reigned, yet, when they are drawn down into superstition, demons and every unclean spirit seize them for themselves, through the bond of consecration . . . Let, therefore, them who have no light, light their lamps daily; let them over whom the fires of hell are imminent, affix to their posts, laurels doomed presently to burn: to them the testimonies of darkness and the omens of their penalties are suitable. You are the light of the world, and a tree ever green. If you have renounced temples, make not your own gate a temple.[45]

In response to our friend Tertullian, I would echo his concern that no Christian should pay homage to idols or demons, whether intentional or not, through how their home is decorated. But I would then assert that the decorations Christians now put up in celebration of Christ's birth are not

45. Tertullian, "Chapter 15: Concerning Festivals."

idolatrous in any way, especially since people no longer associate doors, gates, or thresholds with any kind of protective deity. In fact, by reclaiming a few forgotten symbols we might instead assert that our decorations are explicitly Christian in meaning and origin. Putting decorations up and doing house blessings in prominent places in our homes instead signifies that God reigns and protects here, that ours is a place where his kingdom has come and is yet still coming. Rather than cause us to worship nature, a decorative tree can help us remember how God placed the tree of the knowledge of good and evil in the center of Eden, a tree that stands as a testament of *both* the goodness of God's creation and our sinful rejection of God's good plan for us in the garden. Next, in using an evergreen, the tree can become either a symbol of Christ himself, the cross on which he died, or the unquenchable life he gives to us and the world. Finally, the lights and ornaments we hang on the trees, along with just being for fun, can also symbolize the fruit on the tree in Eden, Communion wafers, and the stars of the night sky in Bethlehem.[46] And whereas for Tertullian and others throughout history these decorations became distractions that detracted from our worship of the True Light of Christ, our decorations can instead become objects of beauty in their own right, because there is nothing inherently idolatrous or sinful about admiring created beauty. As tools drawn from creation, our decorations can help us remember and tell the story of Christ who came to earth and became flesh, the *stuff* of this earth. Despite any pagan associations, a tree is after all primarily part of God's created order. Which is to say, if trees *are* seen as pagan symbols (and it is not clear they are in today's world except by contemporary pagans and nature worshippers) then it is now time for us to reclaim the symbol if we so desire.

To take the second example, of a guilt-inducing Santa Claus, is another matter altogether, and I believe it has no place within the traditions of the Church. While in many ways I am open to having fun with the mythologies of Christmas (as I discussed in the previous section) it is harmful for children's spiritual formation to tell them a mythical figure named Santa Claus (whom they think is real) sees everything they do and weighs their rights and wrongs from the past year on a moral scale, thus turning Christmas into an annual children's version of the final Day of Judgment in the form

---

46. For a thorough but concise history behind Christmas trees and how the symbolism mentioned above came to be used, please see Bowler, *Encyclopedia of Christmas*, 226–27.

of receiving either the "naughty" or "nice" gifts.[47] If Jesus died on the cross once for all for our sins and conquered death through his resurrection, why would we ever tell children that an elven man from the North Pole is watching everything they do? Santa Claus, and all his similar manifestations from other cultures, is simply a false god before whom we must constantly live in fear, and thus is simply not Christian. There is nothing to redeem in the action itself, because it is a corrupt way to attempt to motivate children to be "good." I am going to assume that most families have by now abandoned this version of the Santa Claus story, but to me this signals that the Mythical Christmas Figure tradition is itself fundamentally problematic. If you truly want your child to believe in mythical figures during their early years, then I would argue you need to discern what ultimate purpose it serves in their lives, because you can incorporate the imaginative aspects of Christmas in other ways (as discussed in the previous section).

This would be my recommendation for any Christmas tradition: look at what the action itself is effecting and symbolizing, and then determine if it is Christian in nature, can be redeemed and transformed, or should be abandoned altogether. Just to be clear, I have already done this kind of discerning for any practice I recommend in this book, but you will have to do your own self-discernment whether it be for my recommendations or your own traditions.

Along with all of this, I believe it is equally important for us to seriously consider what false gods from our own age might be embedding themselves into our Christmases, those practices that may cause us to unknowingly fall into idolatry because they *seem* modern and thus could not be "pagan." The most obvious example of this would be the blatant materialism and consumerism that surrounds and permeates nearly all realms of the season. It is the unquenchable desire to *have more* that causes us to enter the temples of Walmart, Amazon, and Target to pay homage to, and adorn our homes with the brands of our devotion. In my own family I must admit we are particularly devoted to the cults known as Legos, Vinyl Records, and Designer Baby Wraps (or carriers). All of which is to say, to the early church, my family's Christmas gift buying habits may have looked disturbingly pagan in their idolatry, even to the point of endangering my soul. To conclude, let us be willing to take a sober look at all our traditions to see where we may have wandered from the path Christ is calling us to.

---

47. Nissenbaum, *The Battle For Christmas*, 73–74.

With all this said, we would do well to consider what it might look like to reinstitute a healthy dose of the supernatural, mythical, and thus "pagan" into our Christmas practices. C. S. Lewis, in his inaugural lecture at Cambridge University, lamentably labeled our age "the un-christening," as opposed to ages past when "Christians and Pagans had much more in common with each other than either has with a post-Christian [person]. The gap between those who worship different gods is not so wide as that between those who worship and those who do not."[48] We currently live in a de-mystified world, where the sciences, including cosmology, genetics, and psychology, make up the all-pervading cultural myths. The most whimsical legends people tell these days are often about how we have been born of stardust, in hopes that we might take some solace either in the idea that humanity was perhaps put on our planet by a long-departed alien race or that through our deaths we will one day return back into stardust.

In being associated with "the darkest night of the year," Christmas was often understood in a similar light as All Hallows Eve, when it was believed lost souls, demons, and a host of mischievous creatures would wander about and torment people if they were not offered a prize or failed to perform a requested ritual the lost souls were asking of them. Out of these beliefs arose the "trick or treat" rituals we tend to associate with Halloween but which came to be established Christmas traditions as well. A multitude of practices developed, many of them hoping to manipulate the agents of Fate,[49] such as this Halloween tradition from Northern Wales: "Each family used to make a great bonfire in a conspicuous place near the house. Every person threw into the ashes a white stone, marked; the stones were searched for in the morning, and if any one were missing the person who had thrown it in would die, it was believed, during the year."[50] Is there anything within our superstitious histories (even within decidedly "Christian" cultures) worth redeeming? C. S. Lewis longed for the world to once again be permeated with the assumption that God is with us and that the supernatural is closer than we think. Indeed, he labelled himself a "dinosaur" for how out of touch he was with the present world's assumed baseline materialism and idolatry of the cult of technology and progress.[51]

48. Lewis, "De Descriptione Temporum," para. 8.

49. Miles, *Christmas Customs and Traditions*, 180–82; and Bowler, *Encyclopedia of Christmas*, 68, 217–18.

50. Miles, *Christmas Customs and Traditions*, 198.

51. Lewis, "De Descriptione Temporum," para. 22.

Here is what I would ask of us as we begin to reform our Christmas practices: how might we re-christen Christmas with the supernatural and mythical without falling into the same fearful superstitions of the past, which have no place in faithful Christianity? In what ways might we portray the coming of Christ as the time when the veil between the earthly and heavenly realms became the most thin, a veil that is perhaps *still* thin, as the Holy Spirit is dwelling among and in us as God's people? And finally, in what ways might we view the incarnation as the inauguration of a great battle between good and evil that culminated in the cross and the empty tomb? The significant difference in our portrayals of the battle moving forward, though, is they will not be fear-based and thus not result in occultic superstitions but in assurance of Christ's victory over sin, death, and Satan. Because of Christ we no longer have to live in fear. How might we make our Christmas celebrations truly more wondrous, more sublime, more *awe*some, in the most literal sense of that word?

Lewis offers two narrative portraits for celebrating in his *Chronicles of Narnia* that on the surface may seem uncomfortably "pagan," but, when placed into their world where Aslan is the savior and true king, their celebrations are in fact made holy. At the end of *Prince Caspian*, during the glorious return of Aslan, Lucy and Susan enter into a boisterous victory procession that includes all the old creatures of Narnia, including Bacchus, who himself is an Aslan worshipper. In this instance, a traveling party essentially broke out in the streets, and as it went through the newly liberated land many others joined in with a mixture of celebration and devotion to Aslan.[52] Their procession had become as holy as it was joyous, and it was one in which all of creation joined in. A similar instance occurs at the end of *The Silver Chair* as Eustace, Jill, and Puddleglum emerge from the underworld to find a group of Narnians engaging in a moonlit midwinter snow dance featuring music, drumming, dancing, fine costumes, and snowball throwing.[53] In Lewis's parables we find that partying is a necessary part of community, that the time we set apart for our amusement is in fact a very serious matter. Sometimes we just need to throw snowballs at each other, dress up in fantastical costumes, and go joyously parading through our neighborhood for an evening of fun. If these are "pagan" aspects of the holiday then so be it, but sometimes the most Christian and God-honoring thing we can do is to enter into some serious forms of celebratory revelry.

---

52. Lewis, *Prince Caspian*, 197–204.
53. Lewis, *The Silver Chair*, 216–18.

This fits into Lewis's entire conception of the cosmos where, as scholar Michael Ward has pointed out, Lewis is forever attempting to bring to life Psalm 19's declaration that "the heavens declare the glory of God" and "their voice goes out through all the earth" (Ps 19:1a, 4a). His stories hope to show that in our own dancing we join in with the ongoing dance of the stars, and that God has ordained and is pleased with them both.[54]

Finally, in light of the freedom to *not* have to be bound to superstition and idolatry within our Christmas practices, how might we rediscover and continue to tell the various myths surrounding Christmas? There are such a wealth of Christmas stories; how might we discern which ones are still worth telling, mining enjoyment and virtuous meaning from them? I certainly have not eradicated fantasies, myths, and legends from my children's literary and filmic lives, so why do so when it comes to telling fantastical tales surrounding Christmas, so long as I model discernment before them about which tales are virtuous and which tales promote a false view of the world? To take modern examples, only the most staunchly puritanical among us would reject the cultural and moral impact of such fantastical and potentially "pagan" Christmas tales as *It's a Wonderful Life*, *A Christmas Carol*, or *The Nutcracker*. All of which is to say, if you are not reading your children *How the Grinch Stole Christmas* because it is a mythical story, then perhaps you should not be reading them *The Cat in the Hat* either.

WHEN IS IT ACCEPTABLE TO SING CHRISTMAS CAROLS?

When I first began attending a church that followed a "liturgical" form of worship, one aspect of it I was immediately drawn to was that it followed the church calendar. What became especially meaningful was entering into the seasons of Advent before Christmas, and Lent before Easter, and consequently how the music we sang together would change so drastically as the seasons changed. Thus the practice was ingrained into me deeply: *we do not sing Christmas songs during Advent.*

Now, there is certainly no universal law or inarguable Biblical warrant declaring you must not listen to or sing Christmas carols until it is December 24 and 25, but it is a tradition I would like to invite you into, most

---

54. Along with his paradigm-shifting *Planet Narnia*, Michael Ward has assessed Lewis's understanding of paganism, the cosmos, and even his views on Christmas in the essays "C. S. Lewis and the Star of Bethlehem," "God the Father of Lights," and "C. S. Lewis, Jupiter and Christmas."

especially if you are a church musician who determines the songs your congregation is singing. As I will explain in my chapter on the meaning of Advent, Christmas, and Epiphany, there is an all-encompassing spiritual posture to take during the season of Advent that prepares us for the glory of Christ's coming at Christmas, and the music we sing together helps us into this posture. So I believe it is important to make a distinction between the music we partake of in our personal lives and the music we sing in our church communities. Again, as there is no real law about this, and I would say people are certainly free to listen to Christmas music as much as they want (even year round!), nonetheless I would highly recommend the practice of singing only Advent-focused songs and hymns in our churches in the lead-up to Christmas.

However, I would further argue that if we begin to more conscientiously choose Advent songs and draw people into the overall spirit of the season, singing Christmas songs too early in December will simply not feel right. That is, if we shape people's liturgical sensibilities correctly, something will feel . . . *off*. Commercial radio stations and retail stores will continue with the status quo and choose to play Christmas songs before Thanksgiving, but when that music reaches *your* ears you may want to change the radio station or fall to your knees and rend your garments right in the middle of the juice aisle. This does not mean we become self-righteous Advent curmudgeons and thus members of the Christmas Carol Police Squad. Instead—and this is something I argue for in more detail in the next section of this chapter,—I believe we should do our faithful best to be reshapers of culture and to appeal to people's aesthetic sensibilities, engaging people in a better story about Christmas. For churches that do not follow the church calendar but who are also considering how to celebrate the 12 days of Christmas, I highly encourage you to look at what it means to also enter into the fullness of Advent, where we simultaneously contemplate Christ's first and second comings. Immerse yourself in the Advent Scripture readings (as according to the Revised Common Lectionary) from Isaiah and other prophets, as well as from the beginning of the Gospels in the lead-up to Christ's birth and baptism, and then experiment with how to invite your community into the story where the people of God learn to wait and struggle and prepare and rejoice. If we can create an immersive experience for people, of which music is an integral part, where the narrative of Advent is more compelling than a prematurely celebrated Christmas season, we will not need to make any such "no Christmas music before

Christmas" law, as people simply will not *want* to sing Christmas carols during Advent because the time is not *right*.

Specifically regarding the music of Advent, there is a wealth of hymns and songs to choose from. To start with, it first helps to realize "O Come, O Come Emmanuel" and "Lo, How A Rose E'er Blooming" are Advent rather than Christmas hymns, which is to say that songs that long for his coming are for Advent, and songs that proclaim he is come are for Christmas. Again, there is no law about this, but I invite you to consider how, through music, you might best shape the story you are telling as a community.

BUT EVERYBODY ELSE BASICALLY CELEBRATES CHRISTMAS BEFORE DECEMBER 25. ISN'T THIS JUST GOING TO MAKE ME A CULTURAL ODDBALL?

I can only hope that the recommendations made in this book will turn you and your community into glorious oddballs that everyone else wants to join in with. Let me be clear: the last thing I want is for you to feel the pressure to add *more* things to do during the Christmas season. I am not looking to make anyone more busy or feel more guilty for not doing enough during the holiday. Instead, I want churches and families to look at themselves as compelling culture makers and reshapers. What would it look like if over a span of years we began immersing people in an alternative way of doing Christmas, one that is coupled with Advent? Because of the current culture, we feel the pressure to have Christmas festivals and concerts during Advent, thus creating a lot of busyness and stress when we should be drawing back, simplifying, and putting ourselves into a posture of waiting, listening, and preparing. My own church does this every December by putting on a large, communal Christmas carol sing-along in a coffee shop. It is a wonderful annual tradition for us, one I helped start, but in my heart I lament that I am not able to be more contemplative during Advent and am instead organizing a multi-faceted event. What if churches began to advocate for Christmas concerts and related events to happen *during* the 12 days? Due to the power of the Christmas Marketing Machine that plays into people's sentimentality and undying desire to buy things, I am skeptical that sweeping cultural changes might actually take place, but I am nonetheless hopeful the church still might be able to shift how Christmas is celebrated over the course of a generation if they risk offering a true alternative.

But here is where we need to count the cost: we should be willing to be more than a little odd and to have our families enter into holiday rhythms that cause others around us to wonder what exactly it is we are doing. Becoming appealing cultural oddities is the only way we will begin to shift people back to celebrating during the 12 days, rather than before them.

ARE THERE ANY OTHER MISCONCEPTIONS ABOUT CHRISTMAS YOU THINK ARE WORTH CLEARING UP?

I am so glad you asked. While there are many disputed and confusing aspects about Christ's birth and the traditions of Christmas that numerous other volumes and articles have gone into, there is one significant part of the Christmas narrative worth correcting, most especially because it has established itself within our Scripture translations as well as how we continue to reenact the story. In Luke 2:7 the English Standard Version reads, "And she gave birth to her firstborn son and wrapped him in swaddling cloths and laid him in a manger, because there was no place for them in the inn." This common translation of the verse has shaped our imaginations to such an extent that it is the norm to depict the Holy Family as wandering travelers in a distant town, who find themselves rejected from the local inn (or multiple inns) as well as a series of homes who refuse them lodging. In these stories, Mary is about ready to give birth at any moment and they end up finding an abandoned stable or cave, and the Son of God experiences his first rejection by the world he came to save, but is then welcomed by humble shepherds and an assortment of stable animals. What needs serious correction is our understanding of the Greek word *katalyma* which is most often translated as "inn" but should instead be given a more neutral and ambiguous translation as "the place to stay," "guest room," or "the room." One scholar has asserted the last part of the verse "should be rendered 'because they had no space in their place to stay,'" or even, "in their accommodations."[55]

The shift in consensus about *where* Jesus was born stems from a growing knowledge about Middle Eastern familial customs and the design of a typical peasant home.[56] To start with, as Luke 2:3 seems to indicate, Bethlehem was Joseph's "own town," and thus in returning for a census there would have been a familial home within his extended family for them to

55. Carlson, "The Accommodations," 326, 336.
56. Bailey, *Jesus through Middle Eastern Eyes*, 25–37.

stay at. It does not even make sense then that they would have sought out lodging at a public inn when it is possible Joseph's childhood home, and perhaps a number of other relatives who could have taken them in, all resided in Bethlehem. Homes at the time (and often still to this day in the Middle East) contained at their entrance a side stable at ground level where they would bring animals inside during the night, which led up, through a set of stairs, to the main room of the house. Sometimes this main room was open to the stables and sometimes there was a barrier wall, but there were typically mangers placed in the raised floor, which would have been at mouth level for the animals. These houses would also have a smaller guest chamber next to the main room or on the roof of the house. This guest chamber is what many scholars believe the word *katalyma* is referring to and their conclusion is that it might have been intended as a marital chamber for Mary and Joseph but it was either not suited for giving birth or the room was already being used when they arrived and was thus unavailable to them. Whatever the circumstances (unknown according to Luke) Joseph's family supposedly gave Mary the main room of the house to give birth in and afterwards laid Jesus in one of the side mangers.[57]

There is a tremendous amount of beautiful tragedy and theological richness in being able to see the Holy Family as rejected, homeless wanderers who gave birth to the Son of God in dire circumstances, but this particular understanding of the text should be corrected and the images and dramatizations in which we portray the story from here on out should reflect this correction.

57. Carlson, "The Accommodations," 341–42.

2

The Meaning of Advent, Christmas, and Epiphany

INTRODUCTION

COMMUNITIES WHO FOLLOW THE church calendar may already have a firm grasp on the narrative and thematic progression from Advent to Christmas, but many of the ministry leaders I know in the Evangelical world do not even know what Advent is, nor how it relates to Christmas. To many, especially music and worship leaders, it seems like the general season of "Christmas" begins either after Thanksgiving (in an American context) or at the beginning of December, and thus there would not even be a legitimate reason to institute legalistic rules like refraining from singing Christmas songs. For a significant amount of us "Advent" is not an idea permeating our minds and hearts. This chapter exists therefore to build a foundation and an argument for why it is necessary and good for us to truly enter into the time of Advent every year before Christmas. Even so, many of us do not approach Christmas as a prolonged season that culminates in the Feast of Epiphany and thus the broader progression of the season is worth exploring as well. This chapter, while offering brief glances into the history of the seasons, is even more focused on providing an introduction to their *meaning*, how they connect to each other, and how we might begin telling their story well.

Advent: the End of the World as We Know It

There is a hidden blessing in the fact that everyone else starts celebrating Christmas right as Advent begins. We should always feel more than a bit out of place during this season, even *dis*placed. We should feel like foreigners in a land not our own, surrounded by happy people practicing traditions we do not understand, while we forlornly long for our homeland. In other words, we should be content to allow ourselves to feel the ache of Advent.

Here are the facts: Advent occurs on the four Sundays before Christmas Day and can begin anytime from November 27 to December 3. The word itself means "coming" or "arrival," and refers to both the first coming of Christ when he was born in Bethlehem, and his future coming when he will reign in glory. A third possible "coming" is found in how each of us are called to know Jesus personally, to encounter him with all of our being. As Advent opens, we find ourselves proclaiming in the first week prophecies surrounding Christ's future coming, the Final Judgment, and the new heavens and new earth, and in the second week prophecies on preparing the way of the Lord and how they found fulfillment in the ministry of John the Baptist. The latter half of Advent focuses on calls to rejoice and take comfort in our suffering as we wait for God and his kingdom to be revealed (often from the perspective of John the Baptist), prophecies surrounding Christ's birth, and the related Gospel narratives recounting what happened in the lead up to his birth.

When a community follows the three-year Sunday lectionary cycle of Old Testament, New Testament, and Gospel readings, they find themselves placed right in the middle of the end of the world. On one year the first week of Advent contains a passage from Isaiah about what God will do in the "latter days" (Isa 2:1–5), reminders that the day of the Lord is closer than we think and thus we should wake from our sleep (Rom 13:11–14), and Jesus's apocalyptic vision in Matthew 24 of the end times when the Son of Man comes again. In other years the first week focuses on God's judgment (Isa 64:1–9), the establishment of his righteousness (Jer 33:1–4), and repeats the other Gospel passages where Jesus foretells the end of the world (Mark 13:24–37, Luke 21:25–36).

In the second week the Old Testament passages dwell on the voice of one crying in the wilderness to "prepare the way of the Lord" (Isa 40:1–11) and shows in the Gospel readings how John the Baptist *was* that voice (Mark 1:1–8, Matt 3:1–12, Luke 3:1–6). The Old Testament passages still proclaim God's future vision for the world where "the wolf shall dwell with the lamb" (Isa 11:6), war has ended (Isa 40:2), the people will be purified (Mal 3:1–4), and the whole earth will see and know the glory of the Lord (Isa 11:10; 40:5). Similarly, the New Testament readings feature calls to be pure and blameless and holy for the day of his coming (Phil 1:3–11), reminders that his coming will be swift and unexpected (2 Pet 3:8–15), and a proclamation that the salvation of the coming one is for all peoples (Rom 15:4–13).

The third week of Advent, known as "Gaudete" or "Rejoice" Sunday, continues these themes, proclaiming that God will cause the desert to burst and blossom forth into new life (Isa 35:1–10), and that he will in his justice repair and restore our ruined cities, comfort the mourning and broken-hearted, and proclaim "liberty to the captives" while giving us a "garment of praise" to rejoice with (Isa 61:1–4, 8–11). The call to "rejoice" as given in the epistle readings of Philippians 4:4–7 and 1 Thessalonians 5:16–24 is a needed reminder that God's redemption is coming, and that even in the midst of suffering and trial God can take away our anxiety and replace it with peace. Though we may be tempted to doubt and despair in a world where evil appears to have won the day (as was John the Baptist during unjust imprisonment in Matthew 11:2–11) we are called to be patient, like a farmer waiting for the earth to produce the "precious fruit" of our labors (Jas 5:7–10). At some point in the three-year cycle of readings the Psalm response is replaced in the third or fourth week with the "Magnificat," which is Mary's song-like prayer in Luke 2:46–55. This canticle from an expectant mother encapsulates in one place nearly all of Advent's themes: that God will exalt the humble and bring down the mighty, that he will fill the bellies of the hungry while sending the rich away empty, that our waiting for the Savior is to consist of quiet, assured rejoicing, and finally that he uses the frail, broken vessels of our lives as the means to bring about his kingdom.

The final week of Advent contains well-known prophecies surrounding Christ's birth: "the virgin shall conceive" (Isa 7:10–16) and "O Bethlehem Ephrathah, who are too little to be among the clans of Judah, from you shall come forth for me one who is to be ruler in Israel" (Mic 5:2). In the Gospel passages, we enter into the expectant unknowing and fear of Mary, and then Joseph, as they began to understand just what they were being called to as Jesus's earthly parents (Luke 1:39–45, Matt 1:18–25). To summarize the words and themes that keep turning up throughout the combined weeks of readings, we can say that Advent is a season of waiting, longing, preparing, repenting, being watchful, staying awake, rejoicing, and being patient and faithful. We see that our God is a God of justice, deliverance, holiness, liberation, and peace, and that he is savior for the whole world.

To be in Advent is to place ourselves within Israel and Judah at the time of the exile, where we expectantly hope for deliverance while living under the rule of another people and in another land. As exiles, our repeated prayer is "my deliverer is coming, my deliver is standing by" as longingly sung in artist Rich Mullins's song "My Deliverer."[1] In Advent we are at the watch, waiting for his coming, hopeful that today might be the day of his return and our lives will be restored, but also knowing we may have to endure for a little while longer. The reason Advent looks to *both* of Christ's arrivals is we come to realize *our* wait in the present is the same as Israel's in the past. The early church, as seen in the fourth week's epistle reading of Hebrews 1:1–12, believed they were always living in the "last days," where at any time Christ could return. We may be tempted to think we are now in another era of cosmic history, but if the Scriptures are our guide, we are to always be in a state of prepared readiness, for we know not the time nor the hour (Matt 24:42, Mark 13:32). Whether viewed as an "exile" or the "end of the world," or shared as a communal or personal experience, the time in the advent before his coming is where we find ourselves separated—due to sin and life's tragic circumstances—from God, people, and the blessed life God intends for us. Paradoxically, in Advent we remember that God's salvation will be fulfilled at some grand future point, but also that his kingdom has come in the here and now and his promised spiritual and physical restoration is for today (Joel 2:24–27).

---

1. Rich Mullins and Mitch McVicker, "My Deliverer," Liturgy Legacy Music/Word Music, 1998.

Often, people who are just learning about the church calendar and the "liturgical" way of worshipping will get confused as to why there need to be different seasons and why the church should be locked into celebrating certain feasts on certain days instead of allowing the Spirit to move on our hearts, thereby having the freedom to choose the focus our worship takes. A few times I have even heard the complaint that it does not make sense to emphasize Easter on a certain day or during a certain season of the year because Christ has risen for all time, and we are to live in the victory of his resurrection every day of our lives. Here is the paradoxical secret that resides at the heart of the church calendar: the person complaining is correct, and for the Christian every day really *is* Easter, but we give special emphasis to the day of Christ's rising, to the season of Easter, and to *every* Sunday as a way of reminding ourselves of this fact. And it is the same for all of the church calendar: we enter into the seasons of Advent, Christmas, and Lent to remind ourselves that—this side of his coming again—we are *always* in a place of expectant Advent waiting, *always* in the Nativity when the Word became flesh and dwelt among us, and *always* in a state of Lenten penitence and repentance, but we enter into the different seasons as a reminder to ourselves that these are the ongoing postures of the Christian life. What we come to realize is that often, even while celebrating the reality of Christ's resurrection, we are called into a place of sorrow when a family member dies, or expectant longing as we search for a new job, or fasting as we become convicted of a harmful sin. Likewise, we will find Easter breaking into our Advents and Lents, and we may find holy cause and license to throw a celebration in the midst of our penitence. Entering into the church calendar means we recognize that Christian identity is simultaneously multifaceted, even while we intentionally immerse ourselves in the spirit, themes, and practices of the individual seasons.

There are two ongoing contentions surrounding Advent that are worth mentioning: first, whether or not it is a penitential season like Lent, and second, whether it is the beginning or the end of the yearly liturgical calendar. At certain points in history, Advent was considered a mini-Lent, as both seasons tended to focus on repentance from sin, and even death and rebirth. Indeed, like Lent, Advent often contained its own set of fasts, which some believe originated as a three-week preparation for baptism at Epiphany, others believe is rooted in the mid-November fast that began after the feast of St. Martin, and still others see as stemming from an ancient Roman fast during the tenth month of the year.[2] Advent is not an officially declared season of penitence by the Roman Catholic Church nor by other traditions, yet the season seems naturally penitential. Perhaps in Lent we *choose* to fast to remind ourselves that God alone is our provider and sustainer, and to also give us the opportunity to burn away the desires and distractions that keep us from knowing God in his fullness. But in Advent we are reminded through our fasting—or at least our intentional drawing back—that *life itself* is naturally penitential, that we continually find ourselves forced into times of mourning, withdrawing, preparing, and hoping that tomorrow will bring new life. Spiritually speaking, Advent is like the period before a party when we are cleaning, arranging, cooking, and nervously anticipating for our guests' arrival. We cannot help but fast as we prepare for the party. If Advent is not penitential, it is certainly a season where we can model before the world what it means to find great joy in holding back from pleasure and what it means to give to others in abundant generosity when we have refrained from pleasing ourselves for a set time each year.

Moving on to the contention over the church calendar, in recent times Advent has been considered the beginning of the yearly calendar, with the year ending at the close of November, with Christ the King Sunday. However, throughout history (and certainly if your heritage is not Eurocentric) the beginning of both the liturgical and civic year has varied from occurring on March 25, coinciding with the Annunciation; in September, coinciding with the harvest; or on December 25, coinciding with Christ's birth.[3] All of which is to say, that our calendars are less set in stone and more adaptable over the generations than we realize. For this reason, I would like us to consider reforming our liturgical calendars by having the church year begin at Christmas, thus coinciding with four annual births (or rebirths): the end of the world and God's recreation of the new heavens and the new earth, the birth of Jesus Christ, the winter solstice when the sun is "reborn" through days of increasing daylight, and the New Year according to the Gregorian and Julian calendars. With the liturgical new year occurring at Christmas, the church can help create a kind of broader New Year's season of which the 12 days of Christmas is a part. The change also makes more sense thematically as we can demonstrate that the church year ends with the literal end

2. Alexander, *Waiting For the Coming*, 8–17; Connell, *On God and Time*, 68–71; and Gunstone, *Christmas and Epiphany*, 80–82.

3. Stookey, *Calendar*, 180, n11; and Alexander, *Waiting For the Coming*, 19–21.

of the world and begins with a true beginning, that of Christ's birth. I am an advocate for this kind of reform, but making the actual change will be up to church leaders and the various authoritative bodies they head up.

As a way of concluding our brief meditation on Advent, here are a few more themes to draw out of the Scriptures, songs, and narratives of the season. First, learn how to emphasize the Trinitarian aspects of Advent. It is relatively easy to note how God the Father moves through God the Son in sending him to the earth, but it is equally important to note the work of the Holy Spirit, especially since the Spirit is present in so many passages, working through the prophets and John the Baptist to bring about the kingdom of heaven and the conceiving of Jesus in the womb of Mary.[4] Next, you might consider how to expound on the rich metaphor of Mary's pregnancy and birth as a way for people to relate to waiting, preparing, and walking in faith into the unknown. For those in the Northern Hemisphere, it might be helpful to utilize the ongoing natural and astronomical symbolism found in harvest, death, dormancy, rebirth in springtime, the diminishing and then lengthening daylight after the solstice, and how all of these natural phenomena have spiritual parallels. A number of churches refrain from saying "Alleluia" and singing the "Gloria," and have no musical instrumentation (or at least subdued music), singing only *a capella*. Some churches also take away flowers from the worship space and decorate with the Lenten color of purple (though some churches use blue to demonstrate it is not a penitential season). None of these gestures are necessarily required, however. Despite the austerity of the season, remember the third week is one of joy because we know our king is coming. Even so, the wilderness-like aura of Advent reminds us that the apocalypse comes in many forms: it can be universal and cosmic as on the Day of the Lord, but it can also be painfully intimate and personal as when we endure any significant life-altering and grief-inducing loss. Finally, remember the many faithful who, in their own weaknesses and failings, prefigured Christ, foretold his coming, and prepared the way for him: along with the heroes of the faith listed in Hebrews chapter 11, we have the examples of Zechariah and Elizabeth, Mary and Joseph, and John the Baptist as our guide and inspiration. The primary way to begin understanding and practicing Advent well is to know their stories well and to know what it meant for them to expectantly wait for the coming One.

4. Connell, *On God and Time*, 75–76.

Christmas: And the Word Became Dangerous and Dwelt Among Us

As a holiday, Christmas is so ubiquitous, so all-encompassing, so culturally saturated and open to endless marketing opportunities that the impact of its story and message have become diluted and neutered throughout the years. "Christmas" is sentimental and saccharine sweet, and we know how to trigger our best filtered memories through carefully selected songs, films, decorations, clothing, food, and a pile of wrapped presents under the tree. Countless books and sermons have been written expounding on the meaning of Christmas (some of which are listed in the appendix of this book) and I do not intend to add to them at any length, but to instead ask us all a question worth pondering: how might we look at Christmas differently and make it fresh again in our hearts and minds? I am going to answer this question for me in the following paragraphs but I would encourage you to do the same for yourself. A question like this is worth revisiting every so often, as we are likely to answer it differently as we mature through life and the years pass on.

For me, I am challenged to see Christmas in a different light when I allow it to become dangerous in my eyes, of which I can think of a number of ways. First, it helps me to remember how offensive and incomprehensible the idea of God becoming flesh was to both the Jewish and Hellenistic world. In the Greco-Roman mind, divinity could take on diverse earthly forms, but not Divinity itself, and though God becoming flesh and dwelling or tabernacling among us has echoes of the Feast of Tabernacles (*Sukkot*),[5] it was offensive to an Israelite to think that God would have a Son of the same substance as himself. Jesus was a threat to the ancient world on so many levels, and his life, from infancy to the cross, was lived in constant danger. Jesus was the world's true king and his coming signaled the unraveling of all the false kingdoms in which we live. Jesus proclaimed peace and forgiveness of sins in a world that only knows violence and vengeance, and in this world Jesus and all who follow after him will continue to be a threat.

Relatedly, the vulnerability of Jesus reminds me of the danger embedded in his birth and life, which causes me to contemplate the salvation he gives us. There is a fallacy in thinking that Jesus was frail and vulnerable as an *infant*, in being born to a woman. Instead, it helps to remember he was *always* frail, and the cross proves it. He is only frail in his humanity because

---

5. Van Loon, *Moments and Days*, 122.

we are frail, yet in assuming our flesh none of his divinity was diminished. We remember that he put on corruptible flesh so that he one day might be raised incorruptible, and that his new body is the promise of our spiritual body to come (1 Cor 15), the first fruits of the new creation. His incarnation was not our atonement, but it was certainly its beginning. The Lord who made heaven and earth exposed himself to the dangers of this world all for the love of us and for our redemption.

The next way that I make Christmas dangerous for myself is to realize that were I alive when he was on earth I may very likely have rejected Jesus as any kind of savior, chosen one, or king. If I were to encounter Jesus as an infant or an adult, I do not know that I would have recognized him or acknowledged him as the Son of God. Were there no halos surrounding his head, no angel host harkening his lordship, no throne of validity to sit upon, what would have been the signal to communicate to me such a truth? Christmas becomes dangerous to me when I realize I may have been too logical, too elitist, too committed to my culture's own way of understanding the world to be able to see Jesus the anointed one for who he was. It makes me afraid to think that I likely would have been one of the many to deny him, and as a result this makes me desperately cling to grace.

One final way to make Christmas dangerous for myself is to intentionally disrupt how I celebrate the holiday this coming year and every year on into the future. This is an acknowledgement that it does very little good to *talk* about what Christmas means if it never leads me into *action*. In our communities we need to be "willing to attend to the extreme cultural criticism" of the combined messages of Advent, Christmas, and Epiphany, noting, as liturgical theologian E. Byron Anderson states:

> The character of the Old Testament readings in the Common Lectionary for Advent just wallops [us] up side the head: "The meek shall inherit the earth," "the poor will be judged with righteousness," "swords will be beat into plowshares." There is this worldview being laid out before us that is completely opposite to everything we are hearing in our current cultural context. Everybody's out shopping but what does that have to do with swords and plowshares, what does that have to do with equity for the meek, righteousness for the poor, healing for the sick, the recovering of sight for the blind? Those texts are just there in our face for Advent and they do not let up when we get to the twelve days of Christmas. For most of our churches in North America, Christmas day happens and we are done with it—we go shopping the next day for the sales. But if

we start to look at the liturgical calendar for example, what is the story we hear in many of our churches in the Common Lectionary the following Sunday? The Holy Family are refugees. Or if we are reading the daily lectionary we get the stoning of Stephen, we get the Gospel of John, the whole story of the Holy Innocents—what do we do with all of that? What do those stories start to do to us if we pay attention to them in the midst of this joyful Christmas season? It could lead us more carefully to some real self examination. Yes, it is a feasting season, but the balance is—the virtuous mean—is that we feast in the knowledge of the Holy Innocents, we feast in the knowledge of Stephen the martyr, we feast in the knowledge of the Holy Family as refugees.[6]

Christmas-made-dangerous means that my perfect image of what the holiday looks like for me might actually be shattered because I am learning how to lay down my life for others in the name of Christ. Christmas cannot remain so comfortable and cozy when its underlying message is to bring healing, justice, and salvation to the world as ambassadors of the Word made flesh. This happy little holiday might be remade entirely in our culture, were it to become as dangerous as that.

Epiphany: A Savior for All the World

The coming of Christ immediately presents us with a question: What exactly does it mean that God has come to dwell among us? Good Friday and Easter present us with their own set of challenging questions—What does it mean that God has died upon a cross and then rose from the grave resurrected?—but Christmas forces us to ponder what it means that Jesus, the Word made flesh, came here in the first place. The coming of the magi at the Feast of Epiphany points us to one major way of answering this question, which is why it should become an integral part of our combined Christmas festival: it is that Jesus came, lived, died, resurrected, and ascended for *all* the peoples of the world. The message of Epiphany, as symbolized in the wise men, is that all the nations of the world have come to Christ in adoration and praise and all those nations can receive salvation, new life, and reconciliation to God through him. At the Epiphany it is made clear that the "chosen people" are no longer relegated to a single nation, but that this humble king of Israel is also king for the whole world. This message is

6. Anderson, unpublished forthcoming interview.

further made manifest later on in the Scriptures throughout the entirety of the book of Acts, as seen in:

The unification of ethnicities at Pentecost	Acts 2
The conversion of the Ethiopian eunuch	Act 8
Peter's vision of the unclean animals being declared clean and the conversion of Cornelius, his household, and other Gentiles	Acts 10
The Council of Jerusalem that decided what the church would do with Gentile believers	Acts 15
Paul's vision of the Macedonian and his subsequent crossing over into Europe from Asia	Acts 16
Paul's preaching in Athens	Acts 17

Acts contains many other instances that declare in word and deed how Jesus had come for all the peoples of the world. While there are a number of other Scriptures that proclaim salvation for the Gentiles, some of which, like Romans 15:4–13 and the various passages in Isaiah, are Advent lectionary readings, a key Biblical text is found in Ephesians 2, which I will quote at length:

> Therefore remember that at one time you Gentiles in the flesh, called "the uncircumcision" by what is called the circumcision, which is made in the flesh by hands—remember that you were at that time separated from Christ, alienated from the commonwealth of Israel and strangers to the covenants of promise, having no hope and without God in the world. But now in Christ Jesus you who once were far off have been brought near by the blood of Christ. For he himself is our peace, who has made us both one and has broken down in his flesh the dividing wall of hostility by abolishing the law of commandments expressed in ordinances, that he might create in himself one new man in place of the two, so making peace, and might reconcile us both to God in one body

through the cross, thereby killing the hostility. And he came and preached peace to you who were far off and peace to those who were near. For through him we both have access in one Spirit to the Father. So then you are no longer strangers and aliens, but you are fellow citizens with the saints and members of the household of God, built on the foundation of the apostles and prophets, Christ Jesus himself being the cornerstone, in whom the whole structure, being joined together, grows into a holy temple in the Lord. In him you also are being built together into a dwelling place for God by the Spirit. (Eph 2:11–22)

The beauty of the Apostle Paul's teaching in Ephesians is this "mystery of Christ" which was once hidden has now been revealed to the whole world: we are all now fellow heirs in Christ, sons and daughters who are full inheritors of the riches of the kingdom of heaven. At Epiphany, we come from afar and lay our gifts before Jesus, knowing that we have been made one in him, knowing that through the cross he has reconciled all people to himself. Christmas and Epiphany are so important because their combined celebration proclaims that the Good News is for *all* people. Perhaps it will help some of us who are still struggling with the cultural roots of the holiday to realize that a major part of the first devotion to Jesus was initiated by foreign, non-Israelite people, that Christmas (or Epiphany) was the first sanctified Pagan holiday. Like in the previous section, the holiday becomes dangerous when we come to understand that the right people did not come and bow down before the Savior—it was a mixture of the lowly and poor in spirit, with sages from entirely other peoples and nations. Dangerous as it is, we become blessed when we realize just how good this news is for us and for the world, and it is our joyous duty to proclaim this news throughout the 12-day season.

It is up to us to imagine, brainstorm, and discern how to weave the stories and themes of Advent, Christmas, and Epiphany together into a compelling series of gathered worship, jubilant celebrations, and selfless service. My hope, for my community and yours, is that our ideals might be transformed into action, and that the kingdom would come through us in ways that are both beautiful and practical, and able to powerfully impact our world, the world Christ came to save.

3

Pre-Christmas Traditions and the Feasts of St. Nicholas and St. Lucia

HISTORY AND MEANING

WHEN LOOKING AT THE type of holiday Christmas is, at least according to its most common traditions, it becomes apparent that it belongs well within the realm of other harvest, midwinter, and end of year festivals. Though we seem to forever be battling about how Christmas should actually be celebrated (or to do away with it altogether!), many of its elements contain fundamental themes shared with other holidays occurring at the same time of the year. There is the common reflection of death and rebirth at the end of the harvest season while we wait for life to begin again in the spring, but also with the sun's descent into darkness as the days shorten, followed by the return of light as the days begin to grow long again. Another similarity between many holidays is a call to rejoice in the gifts that God or nature has provided for us as demonstrated in the form of various feasts, bouts of giving gifts, and decorations drawn from the earth. There also seems to be a shared thinning of the veil between heaven and earth, where God himself or other spiritual beings draw close and manifest themselves to us. Finally, many holidays contain a quiet homebound time for drawing close to our families and communities, but also the possibility for rambunctious behavior where we rebel against social conventions and parade around our neighborhoods looking for some midwinter trouble.[1]

Along with the Sundays leading to the end of ordinary time, the possible number of feast and saints' days to celebrate from October until the end of the 12 days of Christmas is staggering, which is why many of them have fallen off our calendars. Nonetheless, the possible holy days could include, but are not limited to:

Halloween	October 31
All Saints' Day	November 1
All Souls' Day	November 2
Guy Fawkes	November 5
St. Martin's Day	November 11
St. Clement's Day	November 23
St. Catherine's Day	November 25
St. Andrew's Day	November 30

1. Clement Miles makes a few of these points with more depth in *Christmas Customs and Traditions*, 167–86.

St. Barbara's Day	December 4
St. Nicholas's Day	December 6
Feast of the Immaculate Conception	December 8
St. Lucia's Day	December 13
St. Thomas's Day	December 21
St. Sylvester's Day	December 31

Along with those mentioned are a number of other feast days leading up to Candlemas on February 2, Mardi Gras (or Carnival), and the beginning of Lent on Ash Wednesday. Bordering and often spilling over into seemingly idolatrous devotion, Protestants have never known quite what to do with saints' days except to reject them, relegating them to being "a Catholic thing." Nonetheless, in recent years I have seen an increasing need for Christians of all kinds to commemorate and reflect upon the "saints" of the past, whether they be family members, church leaders, or more well-known figures like Corrie Ten Boom, Dietrich Bonhoeffer, or C. S. Lewis, which signals that we have an innate need to remember the inspiring greatness of certain heroes of the faith and to look to their lives as an example for our own.

Two Advent feast days that have become part of many pre-Christmas traditions are St. Nicholas's Day on December 6 (which was already discussed in chapter 1) and St. Lucia's Day (or Lucy) on December 13. As a saint, Lucia gained prominence by the sixth century in Italy (where she was from) and Scandinavian countries a few centuries later, as an increasing amount of miracles began to be associated with her name and people were having visions of a "beautiful, radiant woman in white."[2] Despite her actual nationality, in many ways Lucia has become a Swedish saint, as her feast day is most popular there (and in other Nordic countries) and most of the traditions for her day stem from there. As a mythical rather than historical figure, Lucia is an angelic virginal young girl or woman, dressed in a white

2. Bowler, *Encyclopedia of Christmas*, 135.

robe, a red sash, a berry-entwined crown decked with candles or lights, and who would lead Christmas processions throughout towns or schools followed by similarly dressed girls and young men known as Star Boys.[3] In this way she became something similar to the Christkindl of Reformed Germany, which is Christ Child in English, who started out as a manifestation of the baby Jesus and would visit children on Christmas (to replace Santa), but who eventually morphed into an archetypal virginal figure.[4] As Sweden adopted a number of its Christmas customs from Germany, there is some reason to believe the angelic version of Lucia is a cultural descendant of the Christkindl.[5] The real Lucia was martyred in the early fourth century under the last great persecutions of the Roman Empire (known as the Diocletianic Persecution, where St. Nicholas was also killed), and was known for her devotion to God, her generosity to the poor, and for bringing food to Christian prisoners. Lucia's name comes from the Latin word *lux* for light, and thus her feast day, being so close to the shortest day of the year, has come to be associated with grand candle and torchlit processions as well as bonfires.[6] Her similarities to the Christkindl are not only in appearance but also function, and Lucia has also come to be a gift-bringer on her feast day, sometimes only giving presents to girls, while Nicholas takes care of the boys on his feast day.[7]

This chapter, while suggesting how you can celebrate the feasts of St. Nicholas and St. Lucia, also has suggestions for how you may enter into some of the more well-known pre-Christmas traditions such as putting up decorations, following an Advent calendar, and doing family devotions.

STRANGE TRADITIONS

Will the Real Santa Claus Please Stand Up?

One of the more eye-opening, as well as humorous, aspects in researching about Christmas was learning that not only is our current conception of Santa Claus a relatively modern one, as Stephen Nissenbaum expertly lays out in his book *The Battle for Christmas*, but that there are also more

---

3. Bowler, *Encyclopedia of Christmas*, 135.

4. Bowler, *Encyclopedia of Christmas*, 43, 90–91.

5. Bowler, *Encyclopedia of Christmas*, 135.

6. Miles, *Christmas Customs and Traditions*, 221–23.

7. Bowler, *Encyclopedia of Christmas*, 135.

versions of Santa Claus and other supernatural Christmas night visitors than we would ever be able to fit into a cohesive Christmas narrative. The historical record offers a veritable multiverse of Santa Clauses to choose from, which is why, as I state in chapter 1, I am more interested in and open to telling mythical Christmas stories to my children for both moral and amusement purposes than I am in attempting to get them to *believe* in them.

Rather than taking space to give an explanation for each of these characters, as Gerry Bowler does in his indispensable *The World Encyclopedia of Christmas*, I would instead like to simply give an account of the astounding array of characters, listing only their names and country of origin, and then let you delve into their mythologies and surrounding traditions on your own.[8] When taking a mountain top view of "Santa Claus," what becomes apparent is not so much that we hold to a singular story across the world and throughout history about a jolly old elf that comes down our chimneys to give us presents, because the variations of characters across cultures are far too vast. We instead seem to share the more general idea of a gift-bringing supernatural visitor or visitors, some of whom are benevolent and kind, some mischievous tricksters, and others who are always ready to bring down a wrathful hand of judgment. The phenomenon is something akin to the many generations and variations of a superhero like Spider-Man where a general narrative thread connects all the comic books and films together, and yet we are not able to say each manifestation is the *same* Spider-Man (a concept depicted in the film *Spider-Man: Into the Spider-Verse*).

To be clear, some of these characters are Santa Claus doppelgängers, some are true alternative visitors, and some are downright evil creatures you would never want visiting your home on the darkest night of the year! Also, as you will see, the primary gift-bringer is often accompanied by what is known as a "companion," some of whom act as assistants (like with Santa's elves), whereas other companions are there to inflict punishment for wrong-doing. So, to recap what has already been established, following along from Saint Nicholas, the historical bishop of Myra in Asia Minor, we find a number of alpine European countries having their Christmas visitor dressed up as the bishop in full bishop's vestments, crozier (walking staff), and miter (hat). Then there is of course the mythical Santa Claus. To the Dutch he is Sinterklaas and is accompanied by Zwarte Piet, called Black Pete

---

8. For an even more comprehensive list than what is presented here, you can visit the Why Christmas website: https://www.whychristmas.com/customs/giftbringers.shtml.

in English, an increasingly problematic companion dressed in Renaissance garb but depicting a Spanish Moor in blackface makeup. In England he has been called Father Christmas, in France Pere Noel (as well as in Argentina, Paraguay, and Brazil), in Portugal Pai Natal, and in the Middle East Baba Noel. In Germany Saint Nicholas is accompanied by Knecht Ruprecht or the Belsnickel, an ominous-looking monk dressed in animal furs and carrying a birch rod ready to whip misbehaving boys and girls.[9] After the Reformation, in some regions of Germany, Austria, Switzerland, and by Dutch immigrants in Pennsylvania, the Gift Bringer was changed into Christkindl or Christkind (Ježíšek in Czech), the Christ child himself, but eventually (as mentioned at the beginning of this chapter) this figure morphed into an angelic, white robed, crowned, and blond haired woman who inaugurates Christmas every year. The name Kris Kringle is a later (nineteenth-century) corruption of Christkindl and the title morphed, oddly enough, into a nickname for Santa Claus. In countries like Austria, parts of Italy, and some Slavic countries, Kringle's companion is the horned goat demon Krampus, who comes carrying chains ready to carry off children. For a number of countries the Christmas visitor is a woman, such as La Befana in Italy, the Baboushka in Russia at Epiphany, and Frau Berchta in Germany and Austria. Along with these, there have been female Belsnicklers (again dressed as monks) and women dressed as the wise men but known as Kris Kringles, yet another emanation of that name. In Russia there was an additional robed Santa-like female character name Kolyáda, who eventually transformed into the figure of the male Grandfather Frost who was accompanied by his niece the Snow Maiden. Then, some regions of Poland have traditionally had their own gift-bringer, known as the Starman. Other countries' gift-bringers and Christmas visitors are troupes of creatures akin to ogres, goblins, or mischievous gnomes such as the Jólasveinar of Iceland (containing the Yule Lads, the people eating Gryla & Leppaludi, and the violent Yule Cat) or the Kallikantzaroi demons of Greece and Southeastern Europe. These mischievous and often vicious characters differ vastly from Santa's helpful, hardworking, and cheerful North Pole elves that many of us are accustomed to as the normal Christmas companions. Finally, many countries employ some form of a masking tradition, where people go about at selected times during the 12 days dressed as a chosen animal or mythical figure. Like the mumming and caroling traditions (which I discuss in chapters 5 and 6), groups of people go around singing, telling riddles, and

9. Bowler, *Encyclopedia of Christmas*, 128.

asking for treats and refreshments, such as the *Mari Lwyd* horse in Wales and the Julebuk deer as in Nordic countries.[10] With this brief survey, my hope is for us to see how the universal concept of the gift-bringer is shared among a plethora of variations across the world. While in modern times the gift-bringers have tended to be increasingly kind, jolly, and giving, in ages past they were much more willing to hand out harsh judgment or people found it necessary for them to have a companion that was. Though the mythologies and the idiosyncratic details may vary, the rituals themselves mostly stay the same.

If Christmas myths are neither relevant nor appropriate to your holiday celebrations, then they can certainly be abandoned altogether. For the folklorists among us, however, we may want to take a deeper look into stories and histories surrounding Santa and the other Christmas visitors that continue to be passed down, as well as those that have currently been forgotten. Rather than policing these narratives for the sake of an unnecessary homogeneity, we can instead rest easy in the fact that cultural myths have *always* been evolving into different versions of themselves and that we ourselves have the opportunity to add new adaptations to old Christmas stories, or to write new stories altogether, if we are so bold.

IDEAS FOR CELEBRATING

Hanging the Greens, Types of Trees, Advent Calendars and Wreaths, Setting Up Your Nativity, and Reciting the "O Antiphons"

There are a number of acceptable options for when to set up Christmas decorations or to "hang the greens" in your church and home. However, my recommendation is to discern how to both commemorate the season by setting up your decorations while at the same maintaining the posture of preparation and holding back that is central to Advent. Very simply, this means hanging up a number of your decorations at the beginning of Advent, but reserving all or most of your lighting until Christmas Eve or Day. Regarding timing, in my own family we set up decorations around the first Sunday of Advent, depending on our family rhythms and schedules at that time of year. A number of European countries use December 8, the Feast of the Immaculate Conception, as the start of the Christmas season

10. Miles, *Christmas Customs and Traditions*, 201–2.

and the day the decorations come out. Some people though take a much more austere approach, believing the beginning of Advent is far too early to be setting up decorations. They delay putting up their tree and lights until Christmas Eve as a way of starkly transitioning from Advent to Christmas. This practice, however, might be soul-crushingly late for many people, especially children. Some ways to hold back while we wait for Jesus's coming are to put decorations up, but to not turn on any lights until Christmas Eve, or to gradually build the amount of lights you turn on as it gets closer to the day. You could do something similar with your tree, gradually putting up ornaments, day by day or once a week. If all that waiting is too much for you, then you could still choose to reserve one prominent decoration to light on Christmas Eve, such as a giant star or wreath. The intent behind this practice is to challenge ourselves by modeling the spirit of Advent where we place ourselves in the time before Christ's coming, a time of uncertainty and hopeful preparation.

Organizing a Hanging of the Greens ceremony for a time of gathered prayer, worship, and decorating together as a church at some point before the first Sunday of Advent can help people to powerfully enter into the season. In recent years churches have begun having Hanging of the Greens blessing services, with various liturgies available online, in official prayer and worship books, and other resources.[11] A service can range from something as simple as prayers of blessing followed by the decorating, all the way to something more formal where the decorations are blessed and then ceremoniously placed within the worship space and other places in the church. The possible items to be blessed could include Christmas trees, wreaths, nativity sets, poinsettias, and any greenery or decorations you traditionally use.[12]

While I assume you can take care of a more typical Christmas tree on your own (lights, ornaments, maybe a tree skirt, and a tree topper such as a star or angel), there are a couple of tree variations that can help you be more intentional about entering into the biblical Advent and Christmas narratives. The first is what is known as a Chrismon tree, which is a tree only decorated with "Chrismons," that is "Christ monograms," which are ornaments depicting specific Christian symbols. Originated in the mid-twentieth century in Virginia as a Lutheran tradition by Frances Kipps Spencer, the ornaments are typically handmade and only white and gold,

---

11. Webber, *The Services of the Christian Year*, 153, is one such source.

12. Webber, *The Services of the Christian Year*, 153.

symbolizing "the purity and majesty of the Son of God and the Son of Man."[13] Instead of the random assortment of ornaments on a typical tree, a Chrismon tree might contain:[14]

a cross

Chi-Rho (a Greek symbol for Christ)

a lamb

an anchor

a fish

a star

angels

a crown of thorns

a king's crown

the Holy Spirit depicted as a dove

the Trinity symbol

According to its founder, the intent behind the tree is to progressively tell the story of Christ through the ornaments.[15]

13. See Ascension Lutheran's web page "Chrismon Ministry," http://www.chrismon.org/.

14. Bowler, *Encyclopedia of Christmas*, 43.

15. "Chrismons and Chrismon Patterns," https://www.whychristmas.com/customs/chrismons.shtml. More explanation can be found (such as where to purchase ornaments or to learn how to make them yourself) at the Ascension Lutheran Chrismon ministry page (www.chrismon.org) or at www.whychristmas.com.

A Jesse tree is very similar, except it resembles a kind of devotional Advent calendar using your Christmas tree. The idea is that every day during Advent you have your kids color and cut out a paper ornament for the tree (or you make permanent ornaments to be used every year), and then you read a passage of Scripture or short devotional reading that tells one part of the salvation narrative each day. This would include creation, the Fall, Israel's history, prophecies of the Messiah, and all the events leading to Christ's birth.[16] This approach to Christmas trees is immersive and gives your whole family the opportunity to hear the scope of the biblical story every Advent.

As mentioned above, Advent calendars are a popular way of marking the time during advent and can be store-bought or homemade as well as reusable or disposable. Used more as a fun way of counting down the days to Christmas, store-bought versions often contain doors with candy or prizes behind them and reusable versions contain slots or drawers to help mark the progress of each day. In the age of mass production, store-bought calendars are increasingly kitschy and can contain pop culture brands such as superheroes and children's TV shows. My recommendation is to either make your calendar tradition decidedly fun (thus doing something more devotional in another format) or to adapt your calendar ritual into something more like the devotional Christmas trees mentioned above which builds up through the Old Testament and birth narratives. Even with a more devotional focus, you can, of course, still choose to give out candy as a way of keeping an element of fun and reward.

Another practice that marks the passage of time during Advent, done in both churches and in the home, is the use of an Advent wreath, which contains three purple or blue candles representing either penitence or royalty, and one pink candle representing joy and rejoicing for Gaudete Sunday, the third week of Advent, which draws on the Philippians 4:4–7 lectionary reading. Often there is a fifth, larger, white candle, called the Christ candle which is lit on Christmas Eve, marking his birth and representing Christ himself. After Christmas Eve all five candles can be lit each night during the 12 days. Sometimes the four colored candles are removed and replaced by all white candles, as white reminds us that Christ is the light who shines in the darkness (John 1:5). Sometimes they are replaced with all red candles,

---

16. There are a number of Jesse tree resources available, one of which can be found in the bibliography under Loyola. See also "Celebrate Advent With a Jesse Tree," https://www.rca.org/jessetree. A children's book that works well as a Jesse tree devotional is Sally Lloyd-Jones's *The Jesus Story Book Bible*.

foreshadowing for us the blood Christ shed on the cross. While the candles are often lit at the beginning of worship each Sunday with written prayers and reflections, in your home it can become a Saturday or Sunday evening ritual done with devotions and prayers.

Thought to have originated with Saint Francis,[17] the tradition of setting up a nativity—in some places also called a créche—is typical in many homes and can vary from small sets that fit on tables and under trees to large sets for outside display. Some communities even have exhibitions where people can view a set of elaborate nativities designed by local artists,[18] and nativity competitions where families in a town get judged for the most creative displays. The standard objects for a nativity are the Holy Family, shepherds, animals, angels, and wise men, but one component is essential to making this part of your Advent tradition: build anticipation for Christmas by having the Holy Family absent until Christmas Eve and the wise men absent until Epiphany. You can make a game of the tradition, by either hiding the figurines somewhere in your house and rewarding the person who finds them with a prize or the privilege to hide it for the following night's search. Another variation is to move the Holy Family gradually closer to the nativity as Christmas Day approaches, and then the wise men gradually closer as Epiphany approaches. You can give children the responsibility for how close they should start out the journey of the Holy Family and the wise men from within your home, as well as how far they should move them each day. This is the kind of tradition that would most likely be too tedious if begun at the beginning of Advent, as that is too many days to have to move the Holy Family, but would work well in the week leading up to Christmas as well as on Holy Innocents Day (December 28) since that is when the wise men first enter the birth narrative. Though there are guided sets available with an included book like *Star from Afar*,[19] this ritual can be done with any nativity and done in tandem with your family devotionals, Advent calendar, or Jesse or Chrismon tree routines.

A prayer-based tradition worth instituting in your family and church, is the recitation of the "O Antiphons," seven brief prayers that each begin with "O," contain their own title for Christ, and, using Old Testament references, are filled with longing for his coming. The prayers, which inspired

17. Miles, *Christmas Customs and Traditions*, 105–6

18. One such annual exhibit can be found at http://www.communityfestivalofnativities.com.

19. Ard, Natalie, *The Christmas Star from Afar*.

the well-known Advent carol "O Come, O Come Emmanuel," are to be started on the evening of December 17 and contain the titles:

Wisdom

Lord and Ruler

Root of Jesse

Key of David

Dawn of the East

King of the Gentiles

Emmanuel

While the traditional forms of the prayers are prescribed and available in quite a few resources, you may also start on the 17th by singing the first verse of "O Come, O Come Emmanuel" and adding a verse each night until you have sung all the verses together on the 23rd. Finally, you could delve deeper into the antiphons by reading a set of reflections and poems based on the antiphons, such as *Waiting on the Word* by the poet Malcom Guite.

St. Nicholas's Day

The typical St. Nicholas Day (December 6) ritual of leaving out one's stockings the night before for the saint to fill with presents is already familiar to most people, but for many this has become a strictly Christmas tradition. However, I recommend shifting these practices to some of the traditions more closely associated with the saint, though adapted to a modern context. In times past it was a common daily routine for all the members in a family to hang up their stockings on the family mantle or hearth to dry overnight after being washed at the end of the day. Thus it made sense that St. Nicholas would discreetly hide his presents inside them when he came to visit families in the night as December 5th turned over into the

6th. However, no one I know currently hangs up their stockings or socks of any kind to dry every night. Instead, we have laundry rooms and little corners or closets at our entryways where we take our shoes on and off. So, as a way of modernizing this tradition I recommend putting your gifts and treats either in people's shoes in your normal household spot for getting them on and off (or near their shoes if this isn't hygienic to you), or in socks hanging up on a clothesline where your laundry dries. In either scenario it can be your children's job to make sure their shoes or socks are positioned and ready the night before. Another alternative to this is to have your children set out their *actual* socks or shoes (as opposed to decorative stockings) hanging them up on or placed under the fireplace to be filled. The point is to have them prepare something they actually use, rather than a mere decoration. The traditional St. Nicholas's Day gifts are chocolate gold coins, oranges (a true luxury in older times), orange chocolate balls, or actual coin money. I recommend relegating yourself to this shorter and traditional list of gifts, as they are fun treats that kids will enjoy but it also ensures they will not expect St. Nicholas's Day to be a time when they get any toys or larger presents. In this way, you can still choose to be nostalgic and hang up your decorative stockings for Christmas Eve if you so desire, filling them with larger treats and gifts to be opened on Christmas morning. But for St. Nicholas's day you can instill the expectation in children that they will get chocolate, coins, and oranges. Another complimentary tradition to instill is to tell the story of St. Nicholas giving wedding gifts to the three young women in his village either on the evening of December 5 as you're preparing your socks or shoes, or the morning of December 6, after your children have discovered their treats. There are a number of longer historical nonfiction books or shorter children's books available about St. Nicholas's life, and it would be enriching to tell other stories about him as the years go on. Whatever variation of traditions you choose to instill, it is important to emphasize that he was a person who cared for the poor and vulnerable and sought to help children. As they get older you can engage them in deeper conversations, asking them what God calls us to as followers of Christ when we see people in need (in big and small ways) and how we might give our possessions, our money, and our time for the sake of others, just like Nicholas.[20]

20. An excellent resource for seeing St. Nicholas's day put into action, for older and younger children, is the "Team Klukas" Youtube channel and their video "Jolly Old Saint Nicholas" where the Klukas family documents their family's traditions: https://www.youtube.com/watch?v=Mj_wGr77SaQ.

St. Lucia's Day

Depending on how you focus on it, St. Lucia's Day (December 13) can be a fun day for children to dress up and inaugurate the Christmas season while still in the midst of Advent, or it can be a day to emphasize being a witness for Christ by carrying his light into a hostile world where we face persecution, just as Lucia did. I recommend leaning into the tension of both, making it a day of joy and exuberance, and beautifully Chrismassy, while also tinged with the heaviness of those who have had to lay down their lives for following Jesus and how we too must be open to that same kind of challenging and humble obedience. On St. Lucia's day we can talk about what it means not to live in fear, to shine Christ's light in the world, and to shed light on the persecuted church throughout history and in the present day. Your celebrations can be relegated to your family, though I would encourage churches and schools to begin leading lighted St. Lucia processions, which work the best in the evening darkness, and end with the choral or congregational singing of carols.

As noted above most of the traditions associated with Lucia's Day come from Sweden and other Scandinavian countries. An important factor to consider is how you portray Lucia. Her typical costume is a white robe or dress, representing the ancient baptismal gown, which is bound by a red sash, symbolizing the blood she shed as a martyr. Then she will wear a wreathed crown on her head, of real or artificial evergreen branches, and decorated with lights or candles. Often, a community will make the choice between either selecting a single Lucia to lead everyone, having a selected group of multiple Lucias, or having everyone dress up like her. These options are the difference between making the annual Lucia position a competitive place of honor (which can create a whole set of problems and heartache) or making *everyone* into Lucia, which does not seem as special. It should be noted that at certain times it was not culturally acceptable for boys to dress up like Lucia, which resulted in the reciprocal tradition of boys making their own blue and white hats decorated with stars and giving themselves the name Starboys. They would follow or surround Lucia in the communal procession. For most cultures it should not be much of an issue for boys to dress up like Lucia. For that matter, if you wanted to incorporate the Starboys tradition in your Lucia, it would make sense to have both Starboys and Stargirls dressed with their decorative hats.

One of the simplest, most cost-effective ways to involve everyone is to color and cut out circular paper wreath crowns with drawn-on candles. In this way, everyone can dress up like Lucia in a more scaled-down fashion, even if a single Lucia has been chosen to lead the procession. Some may want to take the risk of going with tradition and have a wreath crown with lighted candles, but it is equally practical (and safer) to purchase sets of portable electric Christmas lights or electric candles instead. Alternatively, you can have everyone carry real or electric candles in their hands, and make evergreen wreath crowns without lights in them for everyone to wear. If you wanted to include berries in her crown, as they do in Sweden, you could attempt to find lingonberries or use the more readily available holly berries. If you are including Starboys and Stargirls in your procession, their hats can be any kind of pointed hat, such as a cone hat or a folded paper hat, that contains glued-on or colored-on stars and any kind of background from plain white to a colored night sky. To complete the St. Lucia costume you will need a white robe and a red sash, either tied around the waist or hung over one shoulder and fastened at the opposite hip.[21]

Food has played a prominent part in St. Lucia's Day and you could certainly decide to offer a smorgasbord of Swedish heritage foods for your family and community, such as meatballs, various pickled and smoked fish, desserts with lingonberries, and cookies. The most common food for this day, of which there are a great deal of recipes available, are saffron buns called *lussekatter* which often have raisins sprinkled on the top and are typically curled into an "s" shape. Called St. Lucia buns in English-speaking countries, they are handed out by those dressed up as Lucia. Making and baking the buns can be a tradition set in place for the night before, or in the early morning of December 13. Some traditions have children waking up in the morning in order to bless the whole household with the buns and freshly brewed coffee.[22]

CONCLUSION

The challenge for Advent will be how to simultaneously engage in parts of the conventional traditions of the season while still maintaining the

21. You can find other St. Lucia's Day ideas and information at: the Team Klukas You-tube video "Saint Lucia Day!" (https://www.youtube.com/watch?v=fIMcMX_66GY) and these articles: *Umgås,* "DIY St. Lucia Crown for Dummies" (http://www.umgasmagazine.com/diy-st-lucia-crown-dummies/) and "Kicking Off The Holiday Season" (http://www.umgasmagazine.com/kicking-off-holiday-season/); and Crayola, "St. Lucia Day Star Hat" (https://www.crayola.com/lesson-plans/st-lucia-day-star-hat-lesson-plan/).

22. Miles, *Christmas Customs and Traditions,* 221.

thematic and spiritual principles of Advent. How might we allow ourselves to remain in the beautiful ache of anticipation as we prepare for Christ's coming, while still joining in the holiday fun going on all around us? Our answer will look different from community to community, causing some of us to draw back altogether into quiet spiritual practices, others to modify traditional Christmas rituals into something more in the spirit of Advent, and all of us to discern how we might transform Advent into a month-long event so compelling that our holiday season would feel incomplete without it.

4

Day 1: Christmas Eve and Christmas Day

HISTORY AND MEANING

THE SAD FACT IS that we have no idea what the first Christmas celebrations looked like. The third-century Church Father Origen, in his homilies on Leviticus, is known for having railed against birthdays as the unholy celebrations of the heathens.[1] Thus, as evidenced by the second-century emergence of various martyrologies (lists commemorating the martyrs of the faith) and by how a saint's day is determined on the calendar, we see the early church placed much more emphasis on when a saint *died* than

---

1. Origen, *Homilies on Leviticus*, 153–75; and Roll, *Toward the Origins of Christmas*, 86.

when they were born, as death indicated their "birthday into heaven."[2] Even so, based on the *Chronograph of 354*, a number of scholars are confident that Christians must have developed Nativity celebrations in the Roman West by the middle of the fourth century (though possibly earlier),[3] and emerging at a similar time in the Eastern Church was Epiphany on January 6, which paired Christ's birth with his baptism, the wedding at Cana, and the multiplication of the loaves.[4]

But again, we do not know what any of their celebrations and liturgies would have looked like (though plenty of Christmas sermons have survived from the same time period). Tantalizingly, the pilgrimage diary of Egeria, the fourth- or fifth-century woman who traveled to the Holy Land and visited its sacred sites while partaking in worship and prayers throughout the liturgical year, is missing a description of "Epiphany" in the churches of Jerusalem and Bethlehem, which celebrated it on January 5 and 6 and focused particularly on Christ's birth and the visit of the magi. Despite not having the specifics of their Epiphany liturgy, we can nonetheless extrapolate what their worship might have been like based on Egeria's descriptions of other times of worship, all of which should seem familiar to us: they read Scripture, sang hymns at various times (sometimes processing out to them), gave sermons, decorated their worship space to fit the season, lit all kinds of candles and lights, and often their worship was an all-night vigil that lasted until sunrise. Apparently, as according to a later lectionary that was a successor to the liturgies of Jerusalem, on January 5 there was "a brief stational liturgy at the 'place of the shepherds,' with Luke 2:8–19, the angelic visit to the shepherds, being read there. Then Matthew 1:18–25, the account of the birth of Jesus, was read in the cave of the nativity, followed by a nocturnal vigil and Eucharist in the Bethlehem church itself, for which the propers were Psalm 2, Titus 2:11–15, and Matthew 2:1–12, the visit of the Magi."[5] The psalm and epistle readings have long been used in Christmas lectionary readings. Two other aspects of the nativity celebrations worth noting were that they celebrated it as an "octave," that is, as a prolonged eight-day season, and that special emphasis was given to the fortieth day after the birth, that is, the feast day now known as Candlemas.[6] Like these

---

2. Roll, *Toward the Origins of Christmas*, 75–76.

3. Roll, *Toward the Origins of Christmas*, 140.

4. Martimort et al., *The Liturgy and Time*, 79.

5. McGowan and Bradshaw, *The Pilgrimage of Egeria*, 88.

6. McGowan and Bradshaw, *The Pilgrimage of Egeria*, 88, 98, 157–60.

ancient pilgrims, we can approach our holy days like annual pilgrimages where we spiritually visit "the sacred sites linked to the life and death of Jesus,"[7] and draw near to the places he lived by retelling the story and offering our adoration with prayer and song. Visitors to the Holy Land "would then carry back to their home churches some of the ceremonies that had impressed them on their visit and attempt to reproduce them there to some extent,"[8] and though the historical record is murky in the first few centuries, we can nonetheless take a pilgrimage, so to speak, to those ancient times, and follow the basic liturgical structures, the Scripture readings, and the general spirit of devotion as they did then.

Generally speaking, what we consider our long-held Christmas traditions are in fact a potentially conflicting mixture of ancient rituals wrapped in modern adaptations. We should all be willing to come to terms with the complexity of our histories, acknowledging that on one hand some rituals and the criticisms levied in reaction to them have always been with us. This would include the condemnation of the blatant materialism and hedonism some gave themselves to during the winter festivals, which even Pagan writers lamented about,[9] but also that there has been a modern resurgence of Christmas since the early to mid 1800s, shifting it from more carnival-like festivities to a holiday centered around the home and family. The shift was brought about through the sentimentalizing of the holiday by means of such iconic cultural touchstones as "A Visit from St. Nicholas" by Clement Clark Moore, Charles Dickens's *A Christmas Carol*, and popular art depicting Santa Claus by Thomas Nast and various advertisements, most notably from the Coca Cola company.[10] As modern people, the task of discernment is up to us. What traditions of the past will we continue to make our own? What newer traditions are worth keeping, which are worth rejecting, and which are in need of significant reformation? But also, what new adaptations and innovations can we offer to our culture as future traditions that might take root now and blossom in later generations? The convergence of these three questions is the underlying focus of this book, as I begin to help us answer the more general question, "What will *my* 12 days of Christmas actually look like?"

7. McGowan and Bradshaw, *The Pilgrimage of Egeria*, 86.
8. McGowan and Bradshaw, *The Pilgrimage of Egeria*, 87.
9. Miller, *Unwrapping Christmas*, 7–9.
10. This is the pervading thesis of Stephen Nissbaum's *The Battle for Christmas*.

Along with two older traditions which we should consider abandoning or significantly adapting, this chapter focuses on how to find balance between the "sacred" and "secular" focal points of the holiday, factors to think about when looking at the group sizes in the events we plan, and finally different practical and theological approaches to gift giving.

Strange Traditions

The Beautiful Error of Las Posadas

Meaning "The Lodgings" or "The Inn," Las Posadas is a tradition celebrated in various Latin American countries and cultures that reenacts the journey of Mary and Joseph to Bethlehem and how they were rejected at various inns and homes in search of lodging. Happening over the course of nine evenings and concluding on Christmas Eve, Las Posadas is a group procession done either within a parish congregation, several congregations in partnership, or a neighborhood. The procession of worshippers is often led by a child dressed as an angel and two other children carrying images of Mary and Joseph. Each night they go to a different house or church, looking to be taken in, but each time they find themselves rejected. On Christmas Eve they are finally taken in by whatever church or home is hosting them that year, and their Christmas worship can now officially begin.[11]

The beauty of this tradition is how it recreates the longing and turmoil faced by the Holy Family. It puts us in their place as weary but obedient pilgrims with no place to stay, a metaphor for this world's hostility toward the Savior and all the disciples who follow after him. The problem, as I address at the end of chapter 1, is that it almost certainly has no basis in history, stemming from a mistranslation and thus misinterpretation of the biblical text. Moving forward, my recommendation to those who follow and love Las Posadas would be to acknowledge the error, but then shift the custom into a "Flight into Egypt" ritual, focusing instead on the narrative of the Holy Family fleeing their homeland and becoming refugees due to the bloodthirsty king Herod (Matt 2:13–23). Though this is an often overlooked section of the birth narrative, it is a section of the story when they were *actually* in desperation and looking for a safe place to live, rather than an imagined one. The ritual could be shifted to some time in the middle of the 12 days, such as beginning on the evening of the Feast of the Holy

11. Bowler, *Encyclopedia of Christmas*, 179.

Innocents (December 28) on up until Twelfth Night (January 5) to mark the start of Epiphany. By starting on the evening of Holy Innocents Day this helps the tradition coincide thematically and narratively with Herod's persecution and how it forced the Holy Family to flee.

Churches wanting to make the Holy Family's plight tangible to their community can make it a point to discuss the various ongoing immigrant crises in our world (such as between the Mexican and US border), and the ongoing worldwide refugee crisis where upwards of seventy million people from various countries continue to be without their homes and homeland.[12] A "Flight into Egypt" ritual makes more historical sense than Las Posadas, but it would certainly be a nascent tradition deserving more consideration and development if it were to take root in a community. However, processional and parade-like rituals have a long history within Christmas traditions and can be easily adapted to different days of the season (as I describe in sections of the next two chapters), and I know of churches who have annual refugee walks to raise awareness of the crisis and thus they and other communities might consider holding a similar event if the correlation to Christmas were powerful enough.[13]

The Darkest Night of the Year?

It is important to remember that for many European cultures with midwinter celebrations taking place around the darkest night of the year—most likely as a pre-Christian holdover—they were believed to be a time when the spirits of our ancestors came back to visit us and the souls of the dead were thought to wander about and possibly stir up mischief.[14] As sunlight wanes with each passing day, "darkness" very literally spreads to its fullest extent, and thus the veil between the spirit realm and the physical world was seen to be particularly thin at this time of the year. The yule log tradition (which I discuss more in chapter 6) was connected to this belief where it was believed that, drawn by the light, the dead gather around us at the

12. "The Refugee Crisis," https://www.iafr.org/refugee-crisis.

13. The annual refugee walk at Living Waters Church in Peoria, Illinois (http://www.livingwaterspeoria.org) raises awareness and funds by giving people the option of walking 1, 4, 8, or 15 miles to replicate the journey of refugees around the world. Similar events are becoming more prominent due to organizations like Refugee Week, which aims to raise awareness to the plight of displaced peoples (see Ghanem, "Refugee Tales: Walking in Solidarity").

14. Miles, *Christmas Customs and Traditions*, 180–81.

family hearth as we take in the fire's warmth on a cold night.[15] Christmas took on the same kind of function as Halloween, when evil forces were seen as invading the world and we became most susceptible to those forces. Thus, as continuations and adaptations of older pagan traditions, in the midst of decidedly Christian cultures, superstitious practices became widely popular at Christmas time.

The rituals themselves had all manner of variations but they shared some general commonalities, such as attempting to find a future spouse, discerning who would die within the coming year, foretelling if the coming year would be prosperous, or locking down what the weather would be like for this year's crops. Though superstitions still persist in modern cultures, they nearly all sound ridiculous to our sensibilities. To take just two examples, on Christmas Eve in England, an unmarried woman would tap on a henhouse door and if a hen cackled her chances of soon marrying were bad, but if a rooster crowed her chances were good.[16] In Poland, families (and their guests) would need to stay seated at the dinner table until a signal was given by the host—otherwise, it was believed the first to rise would die within the coming year.[17] Many other traditions took on a darker tone and, along with the tales that accompanied them, included people dressing up as demons and all manner of beasts and monsters, such as Krampus and other devils, werewolves, the Kallikantzaroi of Greece, and various child-terrifying witches, some of which threatened to disembowel them.[18]

My friends Petr and Gabi Michlik from Czechia recounted stories from the St. Nicholas Day traditions of their childhoods in the 1980s and 90s which are similar to a number of European traditions that occur throughout the Advent and Christmas seasons. Where Petr was from, highly condensed populations lived on housing estates in large apartment complexes. A few parents would volunteer to dress up like the devils and they would follow behind whoever was dressed up as St. Nicholas, going from apartment to apartment and building to building. The devils would often carry a large bag, just in case they needed to put a child into it. As the night went on, a trail of fifty to one hundred children would be following the group, with many children jeering and throwing rocks at the devils, who were hated by everyone. Sometimes parents would hire one of

---

15. Miles, *Christmas Customs and Traditions*, 180–81.

16. Bowler, *Encyclopedia of Christmas*, 70.

17. Bowler, *Encyclopedia of Christmas*, 218.

18. Bowler, *Encyclopedia of Christmas*, 68, 246, 248.

the costumed devils for a little bit of money to specifically scare their child when the group made their visit. While hearing the shouts of the children as the procession came nearer, Petr would "peak out the window and [see] the devil is coming into the house, with the angel, and St. Nicholas . . . St. Nick would ask you if you were a good child, the angel would ask you if you have a song or a poem to tell them, and if you didn't the devil would try to get you into his bag and carry you to Hell!"[19] Petr recalls one traumatizing instance when his uncle got put in the devil's bag and Petr believed he had actually been taken off to hell. In another instance, he once heard about a neighbor boy who wet his pants from fear of being put into the bag by the devil. Petr, who has rejected any kind of tradition like this in his own family, reflects on the possible meaning of these practices: "The old Christmas is filled with fear. It's this coexistence of fear and joy. It's kind of like the most exciting games to play are the ones you can *really* lose,"[20] that is, with the possibility of actually being dragged off by a demon as a consequence for your behavior.

Similar to the jeering children who would ridicule the demons following St. Nicholas, at certain times during the 12 days people would ring church bells, go door to door making loud noises with guns, fireworks, or whips, they would sprinkle holy water or burn incense in their homes, or chain the legs of their family table, all in the hopes that such practices might scare haunting spirits away or protect them against evil forces.[21] One custom which used to be common and some are hoping to revive is that of attempting to scare each other by telling ghost and horror stories around the holiday, of which Dickens's *A Christmas Carol* is the most popular and enduring example and one we forget is primarily a ghost story.[22] Even though we may enjoy a good scary story, I assume most of us will not want to have these kinds of superstitions as any part of our Christmas practices, especially not any kind of belief that gives too much authoritative power to the demonic realm and that seeks to terrorize children with fears of judgment and torture. Even so, perhaps this time of year can be a reminder that Christ came into the world to overcome evil and darkness and yes, to defeat Satan (Gen 3:15). We can put aside the sadistically twisted and fear-based traditions mentioned above while still remembering Paul's words in

19. Michlik and Michlik, "Happy Pagan Christmas!"

20. Michlik and Michlik, "Happy Pagan Christmas!"

21. Bowler, *Encyclopedia of Christmas*, 68, 78, 218.

22. Dickey, "A Plea to Resurrect the Christmas Tradition of Telling Ghost Stories."

Ephesians 6:12: "For we do not wrestle against flesh and blood, but against the rulers, against the authorities, against the cosmic powers over this present darkness, against the spiritual forces of evil in the heavenly places" (ESV). My Czech friends, who have chosen not to include any of the Christmas practices of their childhood with their own children, even going so far as to mostly not celebrate Christmas at all, nevertheless have this bit of wisdom to offer about how to approach the presence of evil forces during the holiday:

> Even the pagan idea . . . of the battle of evil and good, [is similar to] Advent being about darkness pressing in and then the light just coming and winning the day . . . Ultimately that is the basic truth of *all* the good stories out there because they really reflect what God has done by bringing his Son into this world . . . [resulting in] the darkness being chased away by the light, and the light bursting forth in the darkness. So even these ideas that were so steeped in this mess, some kernel of it is saying something about us as humanity that we have this longterm memory that is communal that we have kept from the very beginning of creation.[23]

Just as giving too much credit to the darkness is unhealthy to our faith, perhaps the opposite—not taking it seriously enough—is equally unhealthy. Perhaps by being bold enough to confront the darkness, even at a time so seemingly happy as Christmas, we might even learn how to best celebrate and speak of the coming of the world's True Light.

IDEAS FOR CELEBRATING

Initial Guidelines for the 12 Days

As I have previously said, in focusing on the season of Christmas my intention is not for this time of year to become *more* busy for you. Instead, my desire is for our Christmases to draw us closer together by being more worshipful and more fun, all while managing somehow to feel *less* busy. And instead of approaching the season with the worry of what other activities we could possibly stuff into it, I believe we should

---

23. Michlik and Michlik, "Happy Pagan Christmas!"

be asking ourselves what kinds of practices *should* actually be part of our Christmases. I acknowledge I am arguing for a form of celebrating that will be difficult to achieve in our culture: to see the 12 days as an extended festival where we learn how to draw back as a community and make our celebrating more intentional and meaningful, feeling the built-in rhythms that swing back and forth between gathered worship and devotion, and gathered activities and games. In a culture where our vacation from work is heavily monitored by our employers, incorporating a 12-day midwinter festival may not be a logistical reality for many. However, with every suggestion in the following chapters it is worth considering how the full-time working person might find a way to enter into the celebrating, before they leave for their day's shift, and when they return in the evenings. What is more, if our Christmas traditions become compelling enough, perhaps we can begin advocating for a shift back to the idea of celebrating through longer extended festivals, and building seasons of rest into our yearly cycles.

As Christians, we seem to be always feeling the pull *away* from the sacred side of Christmas, with the holiday becoming increasingly secular, commercialized, pagan, or just frivolous fun. I would like to offer us the opportunity not to get caught in this trap, but instead to allow us the freedom to embrace the secular along with the sacred aspects of the holiday. As God's people who are "one in Christ" (Gal 3:27–28) we can have freedom in the Spirit to know that, unless a tradition is unholy in both origin and action, God sanctifies and even blesses leisurely and fun forms of celebrating. So long as we continue to feel the pull back to the worship of God who came and dwelt among us, traditions such as grand feasts, sporting events, playing games, watching films, and even a general silliness can all be part of a grander vision of what it means to be children of God caught up in love for our Savior.

With these as our base principles, there are two main factors you will need to consider when planning for the season: first, the ratio of worship and service events to fun and leisure events, and second, the size of the social group involved. It will become apparent from the start how these two factors continually intersect each other. For instance, when thinking about how your community will worship, you will need to determine if you will be holding a morning and evening prayer service every one of the 12 days (which most likely would not have many participants), or if you will mostly encourage people to worship at home with their own prayer and devotions.

Another option would be to promote a few prominent times for worship and prayer such as Christmas, the Sunday after the 25th, the Feast of the Holy Name, and Epiphany. Even still, you could try to add the other feast days to the more prominent days as times for the church to gather, which would not add up to the full 12 days. This would include St. Stephen's, St. John's, and the Feast of the Holy Innocents. Depending on how you want to shape the season, each one of the days can feel different, but the social dynamics are worth considering in each circumstance. As an example, a tension may arise between the choice to make Epiphany into a time of worship or a fun time for celebrating. Your church may want to put on a festival featuring carnival games and lots of cake, but it also may want to stage a nativity play and time for worship. It may prove difficult to do both at once, but you also might make it a single, grand combined event (as I suggest in chapter 9). Even so, the "social group" of a worship service and a carnival are similar to each other, and to that factor we now turn.

Let us consider six sizes of social groups:[24]

- Individual: 1 person
- Intimate Group: 2–5 people
- Small Group: 5–12 people
- Mid-size Group: 12–50 people
- Large Mid-size Group: 50–150 people
- Large Group: 150 or more people

Though I recommended against it in chapter 1, basically all Christmas traditions can be celebrated by a lone individual. I suppose you could even go get yourself a Christmas present like Mr. Bean does in his holiday special "Merry Christmas, Mr. Bean." However, most family celebrations tend to occur within intimate or small group sizes, where most everyone can participate together in a single, focused activity. Church small groups or a play group of children would also fall in this range. I had a lot of aunts, uncles, and cousins growing up, and Christmas at our grandmother's house contained upwards of forty people at certain times, and thus it operated as a mid-size group. The gathering was so large that there were often three to

24. Though these groups are my own categorizations, they are in part based on the church planting article "Mid Sized Mission" by Joanne Appleton, and the basic concepts from "Dunbar's number," the social group theory of anthropologist Robin Dunbar (Dunbar, "Neocortex Size").

five clusters or subgroups operating in different conversations and activities all at once throughout the house, though we were still able to gather together when grandma opened her presents and distributed her annual gift of twenty dollars and a card. The same thing happens when my church's leadership has a Christmas party that includes all our spouses and our children. When my children's school puts on an auction fundraiser, around seventy-five to one hundred twenty-five people usually show up and it is difficult to keep track of everyone and how they divide into and migrate between many different subgroups throughout the night. The only way to overcome this division is to gather them together for a school program, where they assemble into rows and are led by a single leader from a microphone. In other words, a large group functions and is managed completely differently in an ordered concert setting than in an open festival.

Taking some examples from typical Christmas practices, if you were to go caroling around your neighborhood or a nursing home, or go on a service project, it would most likely resemble a small to mid-size group, though if you add the residents of a nursing home it would definitely act as a mid-size group. If you decide to have a game night at your church, you would most likely have a mid-size group that divided up into a number of intimate or small groups if you played a number of different card, board, and role-playing games. However, if your game night gathers a small or mid-sized group, you could play one or two combined large group games altogether at once—which is to say that a church game night is not going to come together very well as a large mid-size group unless you find a way to divide up into several smaller groups. Finally, if you decide to do a kind of carnival or bazaar, you will then be embracing the joyously chaotic elements of the large mid-size or large group, but if you gather people together for a time of worship and prayer, you will have a much easier time leading them as a single group. The main things to always consider are the dynamics of the social group(s) you are creating based on the kind of event you are holding, and then that everything is scalable. This means that events like caroling, Christmas plays, carnivals and game nights, and times of worship and prayer can all be adapted to fit the context of your immediate family, your extended family, groupings of families and friends, and then the broader groups of churches and schools.

Keeping the Mass in Christmas

Is Christmas a family holiday centered around hearth and home, or a sacred holiday centered around the church in gathered worship? I believe the answer to this question is not to dissolve its tension but to instead find ourselves *as families* always drawn to joining the larger church as we hear the call to adore our king, and then as *the church* to always feel the call to draw back into more intimate spaces where we care for one another in our families. For many churches, though, apart from regular Sunday worship the 12-day season has ceased to be a time when the church gathers. Culturally speaking, it seems church leaders are tired of attempting to get families to come worship and pray when everyone wants to be home enjoying presents, food, and relaxation. Noting how this is a cultural battle we are not likely to win, writer John Gunstone has even proposed changing the dates of Christmas, Epiphany, and other significant holy days that fall within the work week, so that they would fall on Sundays. For instance, Christmas could be moved to last Sunday of December, which would cause it to be anywhere from December 25 to 31, and then Epiphany could fall on the following Sunday, creating a classic week-long octave of Christmas, which has been prominent at times.[25] Many churches already employ a model like this for Epiphany, where instead of celebrating the feast right on January 6 they celebrate it on the closest Sunday to it. Viewed this way, shifting the season to Sundays would be an act of hospitality in a culture that increasingly does not separate out time for worship and church life:

> By adopting a revision like this, it would be possible to reach larger congregations with the narratives of those scriptural passages which unfold the manifestations and implications of the Incarnation . . . To look at it from a pastoral angle, it is difficult to impress on people that what the Church celebrates at Epiphany or on January 13th is just as important as what she celebrates at Christmas if the observance of these days is possible only for a devout few.[26]

Gunston's argument is that since people already feel the impetus to worship on Sundays and are more likely to set aside time then, we should

25. Gunstone, *Christmas and Epiphany*, 92.
26. Gunstone, *Christmas and Epiphany*, 92.

take the pressure off of them by designating a day as important as Christmas to a time when people are *already* coming to church (or at least more likely to come).

While this idea makes a lot of cultural sense, and might make it easier for non-churchgoers to find their way into our churches on Christmas, it forgets the powerful draw of December 25th in our culture, and seems like it too easily lets us out of the challenge of seeing the holiday as an extended season for us to enter into. Nonetheless, culture can shift over time and perhaps, if someone can make a strong enough argument, we could find ourselves fixing Christmas day, similar to Easter, to the last Sunday of December.

Individual churches will have to make their own decisions about what worship looks like for them during the 12 days. Those who decide to worship on Christmas morning and the subsequent days will find themselves as cultural trailblazers and may have to endure many years of low attendance on December 25, 26, and so on. However, it is worth experimenting with different times for holy day services, perhaps offering early Morning Prayer for those who work, or early Evening Prayer to suit families as well as those just getting off work. A truly ambitious and well-resourced church could offer both. Specifically for Christmas, I believe we will have a difficult time convincing people *why* they should get their families ready for church once again on Christmas morning after coming to church the night before, though we should consider offering mid- to late-morning liturgies that fall in between present-opening within our immediate families and a larger gathering for lunch at someone's house. The challenge remains before us: how do we make worship and devotion central to our Christmases? How do we draw people into the wonder of this feast rather than making them think they now have *more* worship services to attend? How do we allow ourselves to feel the pull to fall at the feet of the Savior? How do we continue to keep the "mass" in Christmas?

Traditionally, there have been four masses (or liturgies) associated with the coming of Christ: one during the day on Christmas Eve and three occurring from nighttime on Christmas Eve on up through Christmas morning.[27] Often held in late afternoon on the day of Christmas Eve, which many enter into as a time of fasting, there is the Vigil Mass, bringing Advent to a close. The first mass of Christmas is then in the evening, often

---

27. Chaney, *The Twelve Days of Christmas*; Filz, "The Symbolism of the 3 Christmas Masses"; and Martimort et al., *The Liturgy and Time*, 83–84.

known as Midnight Mass, and is meant to ring in the birth of Christ at midnight, stemming from a belief that he was born at that time in the night. Because the Gospel reading during this liturgy contains the proclamation of the angels to the shepherds, it has come to be known as "The Angels' Mass." Many churches offer an earlier evening service rather than one that actually ends at midnight, and since the next day technically begins at sundown, many traditions count their Christmas Eve as their Christmas service, finding it unnecessary to gather on Christmas Day. Many families have incorporated traditions based around attending Midnight Mass, such as opening presents at home beforehand, waking up younger children to go to mass, sharing a meal or dessert after everyone comes home from mass, and then placing Christ in the manger of their nativity while someone might read the nativity Gospel passage again. The second traditional mass occurs at sunrise on Christmas morning, and as the Gospel reading is from Luke, where the shepherds go and find Jesus and his parents and then go tell others about him, it is known as "The Shepherds' Mass." The third mass of Christmas, celebrated in the sunlight of the later morning, is known as "The King's Mass," and, drawing from John chapter 1, it focuses on Christ's divinity and rule over all creation. As stated above, churches holding Christmas Day services will need to discern how to adapt their worship times to suit what their people are willing to commit to every year, or they will unswervingly commit to a set of times and then have to be ready for not a lot of people to show up. For those holding a sunrise mass, you may want to immediately follow it with the next mass (perhaps after a brief break for refreshments) so that people will not have to go home. Conversely, you could give a sizable break in between them, holding the final service in mid- to late morning and giving people the option of going home to open presents and have breakfast after gathering for worship at sunrise. Some ways to emphasize the themes of each mass are to have works of art on hand prominently featuring angels, the shepherds, and Christ's divinity, to prominently feature a nativity located in the nave or worship space and then bring on the designated figures at some point during the liturgy, or to have readers dressed up as angels and shepherds who give a demonstrative or dramatic reading of the text. Likewise you could have the reader somehow emphasize the Word of God made flesh, perhaps by their placement within the congregation.

An alternative to the prescribed Christmas liturgies, which can still include the Eucharist, is to put on a Lessons and Carols service on

Christmas Eve, where the "lessons" are typically nine Scripture passages detailing the salvation narrative up until the birth of Christ, interspersed with appropriately themed Christmas carols. A tradition begun in England in the late-nineteenth century and made famous by the annual broadcast of King's College at Cambridge, a Lessons and Carols service can be particularly powerful in communicating the full scope of the Bible's proclamation of the Messiah's coming and our need for redemption. The music can be adapted in a variety of ways, with music directors choosing to arrange all the carols and songs for congregational singing, from full choral arrangements, to contemporary songs for a worship band, to everything in between. The Scripture passages are usually many of the same ones used in a family's Jesse tree devotional, and some churches may wish to incorporate that as part of their tradition, where, once a Scripture has been read aloud to the congregation, a designated person goes and places the corresponding ornament onto a tree positioned in a prominent place in the worship space. King's College publishes their Lessons and Carols order of service online every year, but many denominations and worship resource books have their own recommendations for the lessons, carols, and surrounding liturgies.[28]

The Sacramental Nature of Gift Giving: A Theology of Christmas Presents

Railing against the vice of Christmas materialism is a tradition as ancient as gift giving itself.[29] We lament the holy day's over-commercialization because it forces us into the position to "Buy buy buy!" thus drawing us away from the awestruck worship of Christ to instead kneel before the false god of insatiable want. We entrap ourselves in the endless sacrificial cycle of not having enough possessions to bring us lasting pleasure, causing us to seek out ever newer possessions to satiate our inner void, but finding ourselves once again unsatisfied we look for even more things to obtain. The way this cycle has transformed the general Christmas atmosphere leads many

28. See "A Festival of Nine Lessons and Carols." A simple liturgy can be found in Webber, *The Services of the Christian Year*, 151–53. An Advent-focused Lessons and Carols is also possible, with the Scriptures ending at the pre-birth passages of the Gospels.

29. For more background information regarding Christmas and materialism see Miller, *Unwrapping Christmas*, 7–11, 75–96.

to question how the practice of gift giving is undertaken as a whole, if not to abandon it altogether.

But is there a way to see giving presents as a human act mirroring the abundant generosity of our self-emptying, gift-giving God (Phil 2:7)? Is it possible to have our approach to gift giving transformed and as a result have the manner and form of how we give our Christmas gifts transformed as well? I believe the way forward is to view gift giving as a kind of sacramental act carried out between loved ones (though not an *actual* sacrament of the church). The simplest and most well-known definition of a sacrament is, as apparently originating from Augustine, "an outward and visible sign of an inward and invisible grace." Communion or Eucharist ("The Great Thanksgiving"), the church's most prominent sacrament, is often used as a default example. When we take and eat the consecrated bread and wine—that is, the "outward" sign—we are in fact participating in, consuming, and becoming one with the body and blood of the crucified and risen Christ—that is, the "inward" grace. The Eucharistic prayers of my own tradition culminate this way: "As we proclaim his death and celebrate his rising in glory, send your Holy Spirit that this bread and this wine may be to us the body and blood of your dear Son. As we eat and drink these holy gifts make us one in Christ, our risen Lord." In a way that is difficult to put into words, when we say that Communion is a sacrament, what we mean is that eating the bread and wine is a way of knowing Christ himself, that Christ makes himself manifest through it.[30]

In the sacraments, God meets us at once in embodied and spiritual realities. So what of Christmas presents? I believe the gifts we give each other can be viewed sacramentally as both a sign of God's self-giving love in sending his Son as our savior, as well as a sign of God's abundant physical provision in our lives. The dilemma of the Christmas gift in modern times is that the object is usually an impersonal commodity, a product purchased in a commercial store and put together on an assembly line in a far-off factory after being designed to further some vast conglomerate's brand value.[31] However, if we were to do some reflection, we would see that by wrapping our gifts and placing them beneath the Christmas tree we are in fact sanctifying and consecrating those gifts as personal expressions of ourselves and demonstrations of our love and connection toward those

---

30. For a more thorough understanding of the sacraments and sacramental theology please see Schmemann, *For the Life of the World*, specifically chapter 2, "The Eucharist."

31. Miller, *Unwrapping Christmas*, 55–56.

we are giving them to.[32] The impersonal commodity is sacramentally converted—consecrated, so to speak—into a gift, with the household parents standing in as the priests.[33] Assuming a typical narrative that the presents arrive sometime in the middle of the night when children are asleep, we might say the presents supernaturally appear and the life-giving evergreen tree brings about the miracle. Utilizing the power of metaphor, could we go a step further and say the tree is Christ himself in whom all things were made (John 1:3) and who gave himself to us as the one true gift? This is a metaphor powerfully expressed in the classic carol "Christ the Apple Tree," the lyrics of which I provide here for reflection, having adapted them somewhat in order to increase their metaphorical potential:

> The tree of life my soul hath seen,
> Laden with fruit, and always green:
> The trees of nature fruitless be
> Compared with Christ the apple tree.

> His beauty doth all things excel:
> By faith I know, but ne'er can tell
> The glory which I now can see
> In Jesus Christ the giving tree.

> For happiness I long have sought,
> And pleasure dearly I have bought:
> I missed of all; but now I see
> 'Tis found in Christ the Christmas tree.

> I'm weary with my former toil,
> Here I will sit and rest awhile:
> Under the shadow I will be
> of Jesus Christ the shelter tree.

> This fruit doth make my soul to thrive,
> It keeps my dying faith alive;
> Which makes my soul in haste to be

32. Miller, *Unwrapping Christmas*, 62.
33. Miller, *Unwrapping Christmas*, 63.

With Jesus Christ the evergreen.[34]

Might *all* gifts be a symbol causing us to remember the imperishable gift of Christ's self-giving love? The evergreen tree itself will never be worshipped but is instead a reminder of eternal life and salvation in Christ. And rather than revealing to children that Santa Claus isn't real when they are old enough, we will instead at the proper age introduce them to the metaphor of the tree and its presents, to the glorious truth it represents and which we joyfully enter into when we gift each other with our modest presents every year.

Through selfless gift giving we can sacramentally enter into the greater reality of the Triune God, where God the Father sent his Son and fills the world with his Spirit. We can take this posture of giving presents whether we use a Christmas tree or not, as the tree, though beautiful and potentially full of meaning, is not essential to the holiday, nor has it been universally used throughout Christmas history, whereas gift giving was arguably instituted as a tradition by the wise men at the first Christmas (or Epiphany). Viewed from the lens of the wise men, our gifts to each other could also be seen as a symbol of our worship of Christ. The wise men first gave gifts to the son of God and worshipped him and proclaimed him king (Matt 2), and we remember their proclamation and act of devotion in our generosity to each other, where loving each other is inevitably an act of love toward God as well, and our very lives are an offering, a living sacrifice given back to God (Rom 12:1). All of life is a gift. Salvation in Christ is a gift. And therefore we give gifts.

Hopefully, taking this approach to gift giving will cause us to consider "a more excellent way," to be more discerning about the quantities and types of presents we give each other. This does not mean I will completely cease buying presents from large corporations with goods assembled who-knows-where, as to me this is not inherently evil. It also does not mean I will cease buying my children toys intrinsically designed for fun, because fun, as I note earlier, can be a fully God-glorifying act. But this perspective should make us pause and seriously discern the types, the origins, and the amount of gifts we give people. It should even make us discern *whom* we give gifts to, as the most meaningful and costly presents are almost exclusively given within the realm of the immediate family, between the three

---

34. Hutchins, "Christ the Apple Tree," with adaptations by Chris Marchand.

generations of grandparents, parents, children,[35] whereas Christ's emphasis on helping those in need among us and the Apostle Paul's emphasis on how the body of Christ should take care of itself challenges us to reconsider what "family" is and how it should function within the church. I go into this subject more in the next chapter. For now, let us consider a few options for what our gift giving can look like.

How to Ruin Christmas for Everyone
(or, Isn't There Another Way to Give Gifts?)

In our minds the traditions of Christmas seem so well-established, especially when it comes to gift giving. Though some variations exist, the "standard" ritual goes like this: we decorate our home with a Christmas tree and our mantelpiece with stockings at some point leading up to Christmas day. Then we place gifts in the stockings and beneath the tree either tantalizingly early in the season or the night before Christmas as everyone sleeps. Next, gifts are opened either some time on Christmas Eve or Christmas morning. In the latter scenario, stockings are emptied first thing in the morning to be followed by the grand present unwrapping after parents are dragged out of bed. The intent is that for Christmas morning we buy lots of presents so we have lots to unwrap and lots of new things to enjoy. We want to be overwhelmed by all the new stuff we have amassed for ourselves and for others, a Christmas bounty of abundance that God has provided for us in his divine goodness, as if all God wanted us to have is more stuff . . .

My own family's habits tend to be conventionally commercialized, in that we spend nearly all of our money buying things from stores and online retailers. I can imagine if my wife and I were to make drastic changes in the types and amount of gifts we give our children it would cause a significant amount of uproar, thus ruining Christmas for everyone. Nonetheless, I have a hope to transform our gift giving, making the act itself more full of meaning and helping us spend less money in the process. So, as a kind of communal thought experiment, let us imagine a full spectrum of options for what gift giving can look like at Christmas. Note that these suggestions assume a relatively child-centric giving ritual, though they can certainly be adapted for other contexts. I have divided the suggestions into two categories: types of gifts and frequency of gifts given.

35. Miller, *Unwrapping Christmas*, 56–57.

Types of Gifts:

Option 1: Homemade Presents

This is certainly the most austere option for gift giving (apart from giving no gifts at all!) and definitely has the potential to ruin Christmas for so many families, especially for children who like their brand name, factory-made toys. On the other hand, making the change to only homemade presents has the potential to completely transform the experience of gift giving and receiving, as our presents will truly be an extension of ourselves and represent countless hours of time spent crafting them. Homemade presents can be anything we can conceive of, and can even include manufactured materials that we fashion into something new. For instance, one year my brother-in-law bought cheap vinyl records from Goodwill, cut out the center title sticker, lacquered them, and turned them into beverage coasters. He is a woodworker in his spare time and using those skills another year he made my wife a beautiful jewelry box. Some other common examples are receiving sewn or knitted clothing, blankets, or quilts, a personally written short story, baked desserts, homebrewed beer, pieces of furniture, or works of art. Early on when my wife and I were dating I would record her a traditional Christmas song and an original song every year as a kind of musical Christmas card. Depending on our approach and investment of time, "homemade" can be the superior option for gift giving.

The options for homemade gifts are as endless as our imaginations, interests, determinations, and talents. The heart of the idea is to take time to craft something special for the people we love, rather than to go the easier and more conventional route of buying whatever the stores provide for us. The downside to this idea is that it is not exactly sustainable for large amounts of people. That is, it might be difficult (or redundant) to make quilts for your *entire* family *every* year. Nonetheless, this idea is worthy of consideration, most especially because it draws us away from the commercialization of the holiday, which has ironically taught us that our gifts are not heartfelt and sincere enough if we have not bought a brand name good from a brand name store. On top of this, the practice also has the potential to save us money.

Author and Environmentalist Bill McKibben lays out a more thorough vision for a Christmas of spending less, and the importance of giving people our time rather than more discardable possessions, in his brief book *Hundred Dollar Holiday*. Along with listing many other ideas for homemade gifts, McKibben offers this encouragement: "So the point is not to stop giving; the point is to give things that matter. Give things that are rare—time, attention, memory, whimsy."[36] In an overly busy world saturated with endless and ever-ready sounds, images, and information, these are the parts of life "we run short on"[37] and are the exact gifts we should be giving each other.

Option 2: Homemade and Store Bought Presents

This option does not require much explanation and assumes that after everyone threw a holy fit when you *made* them give only homemade presents one year, the following year you compromised and said "OK, this year everyone has to give at least *one* homemade present, no matter how small, and then after that you can buy something from the stores." I honestly think this is the option that would work best for my family, where they receive something fashioned out of love but then they also get something fun they salivated over and begged us for when those perennial Christmas catalogues found their way into our mailbox. Also, doing a combination of present types might be the best way, as they enter adulthood, to disciple my children into seeing that handcrafted gifts are nearly always superior in every way, whereas entirely taking away the prospect of getting fun toys would only build resentment in them.

The "homemade present" is a tradition worth considering, one that will create priceless memories for your family and build expectation from year to year. One of the more simple and straightforward "homemade" ways to bless your family (and one that can be a document of the years you have spent together), as suggested by author Michelle Van Loon, is to write individual letters to each of your children and family members, recalling the joys and frustrations of the past year and lifting up the hopes and prayers you have for them in the coming year.[38] You could also do something more creative, as did J. R. R. Tolkien in his *Letters from Father Christmas*, and each year write your family a new Christmas story to be read aloud to each other.

---

36. McKibben, *Hundred Dollar Holiday*, 82. Even more homemade gift ideas can be found at: http://simplelivingworks.org/.

37. McKibben, *Hundred Dollar Holiday*, 82.

38. Van Loon, unpublished forthcoming interview.

Option 3: Buying From Locally Owned Stores or Small Businesses That Make Their Own Products.

As with option 1, the choices here are almost endless, depending on your budget and where you know to shop. In my own city there are a few stores that sell uniquely made crafts and home goods. We have vintage clothing stores, used record and book shops, and a surprisingly high amount of artists and artisans from whom we can commission a work of our choosing. And all of the options available in my own city are also available online, but on a vastly grander scale, where we can find handcrafted jewelry, musical instruments, and yes even children's toys. Do some searches among your friends or generally online and you will find an overwhelming amount of wonderful gifts for your loved ones, assuming you can afford them, because some can be quite expensive. This approach to gift giving is also intentionally more personal while still being enmeshed in the commercial world, as it supports individual artisans and small business owners, some of whom are our friends and neighbors.

Option 4: Give an Experience

One approach to giving that has gained momentum in recent years is to give people an experience which they can enjoy over a prolonged period of time. Some ideas are year-long memberships to a museum, nature park, or theme park, season tickets to a sports team, symphony, or drama company, a set of music or art lessons, or any kind of fun experience like going to a restaurant, getting a massage, rock climbing, skiing, or a helicopter ride. As with option 2 this approach could be a hybrid where perhaps one third of your gift budget could be spent on something experiential. A cheaper version of this is to write out or print your own certificates and gift people your time, talents, and services, such as an afternoon at a park, a back massage, any kind of household chore or repair, a date night with your spouse, babysitting, petsitting, or whatever ways you can gift loved ones with your time and service. As always, there are many possible choices in this category, but it is entirely up to you how much of a Christmas present disruptor you want to be!

Option 5: Giving to Charities and Ministries

Speaking of disrupting, there is of course the option of not buying any presents at all (or to come close to doing so) and to instead, either within your family or community group, give to a worthy cause. The possibilities of charities, ministries, and "causes" to give to is naturally overwhelming, so it is worth discerning where there is the most need in your community or the larger world and from there where God is leading you all to help. There are websites that can help you discern the most reputable charities and organizations like "Charity Watch," "The Life You Can Save," "Give," and "Charity Navigator."[39] Thinking more locally, you can develop a relationship with a local ministry or charity, which would have a more direct impact in an area of need, and at the same time you would know exactly what you are giving your money and time to. Giving can also be intentionally personal and you or your church can set aside money throughout the year to give to families you know are in need during the holidays, so long as the giving maintains their dignity and is not used to bring attention to yourselves. Of course you can practice this *out*ward form of giving while still getting presents for your family and friends. But all of these options are laid before you as a means of discernment: in light of the coming of Christ, how is God calling us to give gifts in the world, both within the smaller circle of our families and in the larger world?

Frequency of Gifts Given

Option 1: The Old Christmas Day (or Eve) Standard

The unwrapping tradition I grew up with was pretty conventional. At one point we opened presents from "mom and dad" on Christmas Eve, with the presents from "Santa" being opened on Christmas morning. In my post-Santa years we abandoned the Christmas Eve tradition altogether. In many ways I see no reason to change this tradition, even for my own family (which, remember, does not incorporate any Santa Claus rituals), except for one key factor: the *amount* of gifts given. Here is my proposal:

What if we gave children (and even adults) one larger, more expensive present, one smaller present, and then whatever fun inexpensive gifts we decide to put into our stockings? The reasoning behind this approach is to

39. Note that all of these organizations' websites end in ".org."

set agreed-upon standards that are fair to everyone and that also build consistent expectations for gift quantities from year to year. In many families, children expect to receive a vast amount of presents and they go from gift to gift, barely comprehending and surely not savoring each of their gifts. By concertedly limiting the number of presents we will hopefully teach them to cherish and focus on what presents they are given.

Whatever our approach, it is important to be intentional about the number of gifts and the amount we spend on each other. Bill McKibben recommended spending only one hundred dollars for the entirety of Christmas, which he actually admits was more of a clever title rather than an exact amount to adhere to.[40] With the inflation of prices and a fluctuating economy, limiting ourselves to one hundred dollars may not be remotely realistic, which is why McKibben eventually leaves the amount we spend up to our own discernment.[41]

Option 2: The 12 Days of Giftmas

An option for gift giving that I have really only heard as a suggestion is to give a present on each of the 12 days. This scenario resembles how some Jewish families celebrate Hanukkah, where a gift is given each of the eight days of the feast. A downside to this approach is the need to have to obtain twelve individual presents for your children or whoever you are giving gifts to, while an upside is that it teaches patience, builds expectation, and brings continuity to the season. To take away the pressure of needing so many gifts, one option is to give larger presents on Christmas Day and Epiphany (as option 3 recommends) and then give smaller and more repeatable gifts on the days in between, such as treats, clothing, or a book. Another option, similar to giving an experience, is to offer homemade gift certificates, and plan surprise events such as saying it's Movie Day, Game Day, Cookie Baking Day, or whatever fun activity you can plan. Though it takes logistical planning, you could also build gifts from relatives into the other days, such as one grandma and grandpa giving their presents on day two of Christmas and the other grandparents give theirs on day three. Finally, and this comes from the Hanukkah tradition of giving gelt, is to give money, such as one

40. McKibben, *Hundred Dollar Holiday*, 13.

41. McKibben, *Hundred Dollar Holiday*, 73–74.

dollar a day or to increase the gift by one dollar a day ending with twelve dollars on January 5, which admittedly could get pricey.[42]

Option 3: On Christmas and Epiphany

For families who are wanting to put more emphasis on the Feast of Epiphany it is worth considering also giving your larger presents on the two most important days, December 25th for Christmas and the evening of January 5th for Twelfth Night or the 6th to focus more on Epiphany. The inauguration of the season on Christmas Day and then its culmination on Epiphany can be given more emphasis by being labeled as gift-giving days in the minds of your children, and you can choose whether your Christmas gifts will be larger, lesser, or equal in value to your Epiphany gifts. Similar to option 2, you could still give presents on each of the 12 days, but then on Christmas and Epiphany you give your larger presents.

As a way of wrapping up this section (pun intended), it is worth considering the gift-giving guidelines of two groups looking to be Christmas-present reformers. SCROOGE, or the Society to Curtail Outrageous and Ostentatious Gift Exchanges, recommends these four main principles:[43]

1. Try to avoid giving (and receiving) extremely expensive gifts, particularly the heavily advertised fad/status symbol items that are often not very useful or practical.

2. Make every effort to use cash rather than credit cards to pay for the items that you do purchase.

3. Emphasize gifts that involve thought and originality, such as handicraft items that you make yourself.

4. Celebrate and enjoy the holidays but remember that a Merry Christmas is not for sale in any story for any amount of money.

The other organization is Simple Living Works! which has an extensive archive of alternative ways to celebrate Christmas, but offers these condensed guidelines for gift giving:[44]

---

42. Rosenstock, "Hanukkah Gifts," para. 3–8.

43. SCROOGE, http://www.oocities.org/enchantedforest/palace/4079/#Principles.

44. Simple Living Works! https://simpleliving.startlogic.com/indexoth.php?place =archives/MR/10tips.php.

1. Plan ahead. Instead of going on auto-pilot the day after Thanksgiving, hold a family meeting to decide what the group really wants to do and who is going to do what.

2. Avoid debt and refuse to be pressured by advertising to overspend.

3. Avoid stress. Don't assume that things have to be the same as they've been in previous years.

4. Draw names rather than everybody giving something to everyone else in your giving circle. Set a ceiling on what can be spent for each gift recipient. Give children one thing they really want, rather than an overload of so many presents.

5. Put gifts under the tree shortly before opening them and then take turns unwrapping so that each item can be admired and each giver thanked. This avoids the tear-off-the-paper frenzy of greed that starts youngsters out on the wrong foot regarding materialism.

6. Perhaps most important, make changes slowly but persistently. Don't try to change everything and everybody all at once. The resistance may make you feel defeated and depressed.

I particularly like how their first and last recommendations might be combined: first, we should do our best to communicate to our family members and to plan together what the best approach to gift-giving is. Next, realize that making changes in our gift habits will inevitably be a disruptor to our established system and almost certainly cause confusion and hurt, and thus it is worth being patient with people and setting realistic expectations from year to year. If we make changes in our habits gradually and as a community, we are more likely to see lasting changes within our local circles of influence and perhaps even within the broader culture.

Miscellaneous Suggestions

While they did not exactly fit in the more general categories of this chapter, it is worth considering these suggestions for what traditions and routines you can build into the 24th and 25th of December:

- In the days leading up to Christmas, or on the Eve of it as you are getting your house ready, give each child their own responsibility when it comes to cleaning and organizing, finishing decorations, gift wrapping, preparing food, or whatever else needs to get done. Give everyone in the house ownership by giving them their own task(s) to be responsible for.[45]

- Bethlehem means "house of bread," and thus, as a reminder of the town that first housed Christ the Bread of Life, and of the Communion bread we partake of in church, it has become traditional to bake a special kind of Christmas bread, of which there are many varieties to choose from.[46]

- You may have traditional familial and cultural foods that you want to be part of your meals, however it is worth making it a tradition each year to try different Christmas foods from around the world. Whether it is a main course, a side dish, a holiday bread, or a tasty dessert, there are an abundance of food traditions worth exploring from all over the world that can be found in holiday cookbooks and also at the website "Why Christmas."

- The symbolism of the manger can be brought into the home with straw, as some countries place it either on the dinner table as a centerpiece or underneath the table on the floor. Straw could also be used as a general decoration anywhere in the house.[47]

- Although there is a similar tradition for Epiphany, you can make a cake for Christmas. If your children are young enough—since it is cheesy—you could decorate the cake saying "Happy Birthday Jesus" and then purchase a set of small Nativity figures, placing them either on top or inside of the cake. For the latter option, the children who discover one of the figurines can win a special prize or gift, which mirrors a prominent Epiphany tradition. This cake can be what you eat on Christmas Eve after church or anytime throughout Christmas Day.[48]

- One liturgical element worth adding to your gathered worship (assuming there is freedom to do so within your tradition) is to mirror some of the language used in the prayers and proclamations of Easter. As a compliment to the Easter proclamation "Christ is risen! He is risen indeed! Alleluia! Alleluia!" your Christmas proclamation can

---

45. Chaney, *The Twelve Days of Christmas*, "The Vigil of Christmas."
46. Chaney, *The Twelve Days of Christmas*, "Christmas Cookery."
47. Chaney, *The Twelve Days of Christmas*, "Christmas Eve Supper."
48. Ackerman and Ackerman, *To God Be the Glory*, 151

be "Christ is born! He is born indeed! Alleluia! Alleluia!" Without making significant changes it is worth considering how other liturgical parallels, in both actions and wording, can be made between the different seasons of the year.

- As part of an "introverted" Christmas, which I discuss with more depth in chapter 6, you could incorporate the Icelandic tradition of "jólabókaflód," pronounced "yo-la-bok-a-flot" and translated as "Yule Book Flood."[49] The tradition is simple and is geared for contemplative introverts seeking to recuse themselves from the social bustle of family and corporate gatherings. In Iceland, a country which values both high rates of literacy and book publishing, a majority of the year's new books are released in the final months of the year, people are encouraged to buy books as presents to be given on Christmas Eve, and then everyone proceeds to spend the rest of the evening reading their new books in cozy comfort. You can of course read out loud to each other, but it might be more fun for everyone to tuck themselves away in a secluded corner of the house and get as much reading done before dozing off to sleep.

49. de la Mare, "Jolabokaflod." This article contains further explanation and history about the tradition, as well as other ideas to incorporate into it

5

Day 2: Feast of St. Stephen and Boxing Day (December 26)

History and Meaning

December 26 is St. Stephen's Day, also called the Feast of St. Stephen, which commemorates the life and death of Stephen, a leader in the early church, whose brief biblical account can be found in the book of Acts in chapters 6–8. Not long after the day of Pentecost, trouble arose for the church in Jerusalem, where the food-needs of the widows among them were being neglected. The Apostles, in order to continue to devote themselves to preaching, to "prayer and the ministry of the word," elected "seven men of good repute" to serve the physical and practical needs of the community (Acts 6:2, 4). These were the first deacons of the church. The Apostles prayed and laid hands on them, anointing and ordaining them for the task (6:6). The first person named in the list of deacons was Stephen, a man "of good repute, full of the Spirit and of wisdom" and "a man full of faith and of the Holy Spirit" (6:3, 5). Stephen, who "was doing great wonders and signs among the people" (6:8) became a defender of the Way of Jesus, and rose up to boldly debate various oppositional groups who wanted to destroy the church for causing so much disruption in Jerusalem. These groups even went so far as to spread lies among the people, specifically about Stephen himself. Though a deacon, and thus by function not a teacher, Stephen proved to be a masterful orator when he was brought before the council and accused of saying Jesus would both destroy the temple and change the Law of Moses (6:14). After giving a powerful speech detailing Israel's history of repeatedly rejecting the prophets God sends them, arguing that the Living God could never be contained by a single worship space (that is, the temple), and then finally accusing the council of being a "stiff-necked people, uncircumcised in heart and ears," who "resist the Holy Spirit," and who "betrayed and murdered" Jesus, the anger of the people was stirred up, and they brought him out of the city, took up stones, and killed him (7:51–60). Earlier on in this account, Luke, the author of Acts, records that everyone on the council "saw that his face was like the face of an angel" (6:15) and even as he died Stephen cried out to God that this sin of murder would not be held against those killing him.

In dying, Stephen became the first martyr of the church era, and thus has been given the title Protomartyr. As a deacon and servant of the church, we remember on his feast day that in Christ we are all called to service and to lay down our lives for our brothers and sisters. Sometimes that means giving up our own time and physical needs and wants, and sometimes, as in the case of Stephen, it means actually having to die for being associated with Christ. And thus, bound up in December 26, right after having celebrated the birth of Christ, there is a reminder that we are to take up our crosses and follow him, that our glory is in humble obedience and servant-hearted love toward others.

Though the date has shifted throughout history, the church has apparently been commemorating Stephen's day since the fifth century, as detailed in the diary of Egeria, who gave her account of the worship cycles of the

Jerusalem church.[1] In states of the British Commonwealth it has come to be known as Boxing Day, a name with a few potential origins. One possibility is that it refers to the "earthenware boxes" of "medieval servants and apprentices" which they would use during the Christmas season to ask for tips from their employers' customers.[2] The "box" could also refer to similar collection boxes placed on sailing ships that a priest would bless and distribute,[3] as well as the benevolence or alms boxes that many churches would include in their buildings to collect offerings for the needy throughout the year (or the season) and then to be opened around Christmas or on the 26th. Though its origin is unclear, there is some consensus that this ritual came out of a pre-Christian Roman practice to put out a collection box at the beginning of the year on or around each village's altar of worship.[4] Sometimes though, people would carry around their own boxes asking for "donations," and here the practice can be seen as a combination of a socially acceptable form of begging, mixed with the idea that workers deserve a Christmas bonus for all the hard work they do throughout the year. The necessity to ask for money at this time of year was for some workers a way to survive the harsh winter months when jobs were sparse, for others it was a means of absolute survival as their jobs did not pay enough, and then for some it was a way to have just enough extra to be able to buy presents and food for a special Christmas meal. When it first developed, this practice was unregulated, which led to many people carrying around boxes all at once and soliciting everyone they met for a donation, including fellow working-class peers. Eventually the nuisance became too much for local authorities and the custom either fell out of practice or was banned in most places.[5] The disparity between the upper and lower classes became glaringly evident in the fact that the 26th came to be when working class people were given the day off and when wealthier families would "bless" their servants and staff with nonreciprocal Christmas gifts.[6] Relatedly, there are other accounts that the "boxes" of the day came from a practice in wealthier homes which referred to the boxed lunches servants would prepare for their masters out of the leftover food from the previous day's feasting. This enabled them to take

1. Talley, *The Origins of the Liturgical Year*, 55.

2. Bowler, *Encyclopedia of Christmas*, 27.

3. Hervey, *The Book of Christmas*, 303.

4. Ashton, *A Righte Merrie Christmasse*, 439.

5. Bowler, *Encyclopedia of Christmas*, 27–28.

6. Hervey, *The Book of Christmas*, 304.

the day off from work and ensured that their employers had something to eat on the 26th, as the aristocracy certainly could not prepare food for themselves![7] It is worth noting, however, that at times throughout history other days were associated with giving to the poor, such as St. Thomas's Day (December 21) in England when those in need would come to the local church and receive flour for their Christmas baking or a small meal packaged for them to take home and be shared.[8] The idea of Christmas giving occurring throughout the season rather than on a single day is an important concept worth practicing in our lives and one I will delve into later in this chapter in the section on a better way to give at Christmas.

In modern times Boxing Day has come to be associated with enjoying televised sporting events, as in Australia, lots of frenzied post-Christmas shopping, as in Canada, or attending or participating in a "panto" which is short for pantomime performance, as in England (for more information on Pantomimes see chapter 6).[9] Finally, though obscure to most cultures (and thus likely to not make a resurgence as traditions), historically St. Stephen's day was associated with two presumably pre-Christian animal rituals. The first, occurring in various European nations, is that of honoring, blessing, racing, and feeding special food to horses, as Stephen somehow became the patron saint of horses, perhaps being confused with another St. Stephen of history.[10] The other tradition, whose origin is rather murky, involved the hunting, killing, and parading of a wren (sometimes real and sometimes fake) by masked and costumed paraders in Ireland.[11]

"Good King Wenceslas" is a popular carol people may not realize was written for St. Stephen's Day and reflects its historical posture toward Christian charity. Written in the middle of the nineteenth century by hymn translator and writer John Mason Neale using a tune from the fourteenth century, it tells the story of the tenth-century Bohemian (that is, Czech) duke Wenceslas (or Václav). In it he looks out his window "on the feast of Stephen," notices a peasant gathering wood for food and warmth, and then, with his servant, follows after the supposedly needy man in order to bless him with meat, wine, and pine logs for his fire.[12] Though not based on

7. Ackerman and Ackerman, *To God Be the Glory*, 151.

8. Baker, *Discovering Christmas Customs*, 15–16.

9. Bowler, *Encyclopedia of Christmas*, 28.

10. Miles, *Christmas Customs and Traditions*, 311–12.

11. Hervey, *The Book of Christmas* 311–13.

12. Keyte, *The New Oxford Book of Carols*, 352–53.

specific accounts about Wenceslas during his lifetime, the carol is rooted in the monarch's strong Christian faith and in his being known for blessing the needy with gifts in the middle of the night.[13] Soon after being tragically assassinated at the hands of his brother, who desired his throne, Wenceslas was canonized as a saint, becoming the patron saint of the Czech people, and having in Prague a famous square named after him, which has been the locus of a number of important historical events in the nation.[14] Neale's carol culminates by focusing on how the selfless love of the saintly monarch compelled him onward through the cold winter's night. Indeed, his very steps were warm ("heat was in the very sod"), making it easier for his servant to follow him in the snow. The message of the carol is made explicit in Neale's conclusion: "Therefore, Christian men, be sure, / Wealth or rank possessing, / Ye who now will bless the poor, / Shall yourselves find blessing." Following in the footsteps of both Wenceslas and Stephen, we too are to live serving others in the name of Christ.

Since Stephen's Day commemorates the life, death, and witness of the saint, the suggestions I give below will primarily focus on ways churches and families can serve their communities and strive to address long-term issues surrounding the giving of money and time to charities and ministries, both local and global. I will not legislate away your opportunity to have a Boxing Day filled with shopping, sports, and lying about the house, but I do believe Stephen's Day is our opportunity to address what service and ministry work, both small and large, might look like during the 12 days and surrounding season.

STRANGE TRADITIONS

The Problem with Saints' Days Is . . .

Though not necessarily "strange," the saints' days of the church calendar year do present a few problems for worshipping communities as the practice has at the very least become a foreign tradition. As mentioned in chapter 3, along with the Protestant quarrel that devotion to the saints inevitably transforms into a kind of worship, idolatry, superstition, or at the very least an *inordinate* amount of devotion (a complex matter worth exploring, but not in this space), saints' days present us with two other problems: first, that

13. Lawson-Jones, *Why Was the Partridge in the Pear Tree?* 116–17.

14. Lawson-Jones, *Why Was the Partridge in the Pear Tree?* 118, 113–14.

there seem to be so many variations as to when each saint's day actually occurs, and second, a lack of personal connection between the common worshipper and the myriad of saints available for commemoration.

The first problem leads to a significant amount of confusion and makes it impossible for a singular calendar to be shared amongst all the major traditions of the church. Looking back into history, we see that saints' days grew out of devotion to martyrs on the day of their deaths (remembering from an earlier chapter the concept of a "heavenly birthday") and eventually expanded to other church leaders the faithful thought worth commemorating.[15] Also, early on, celebrations seemed to be confined to the city where the saint died, where they were from, or where their bones resided and over which a church, known as martyriums, had been built in their honor. Eventually, various calendars attempting to give accurate accounts of the feast days were formed and the saints began to be celebrated all over Christendom and not only limited to geographical proximity. The result of different traditions and ecclesial decision-making bodies is that even today there are significant variances in the calendars of the Eastern and Western churches. As examples, Stephen's Day is on December 26 in Western churches but on the 27th in Eastern Orthodox churches, and Holy Innocents Day is on December 28 in the West but the 29th in the East. There are also a number of Eastern feasts and commemorations during the 12 days not even celebrated in the West.[16]

It may be frustrating having so many possible variations as to when each feast day in fact is, but ultimately we must leave it up to our traditions to determine who or what will be celebrated on a given day, or we must be willing to take up the challenge of seeking to work within and across traditions to reform and align our separate calendars. For example, during the Second Vatican Council the Roman Church decided to once again make January 1st, going back to an older tradition, the Solemnity of Mary as Mother of God. However, since Jesus was circumcised and named on the eighth day after his birth and January 1st is eight days after Christmas Day, it makes little sense for the 1st to be anything but the circumcision and

15. Bradshaw and Johnson, *The Origins of Feasts*, 174. Two excellent summaries on the development of devotion to saints and the calendars that formed as a result can be found in Bradshaw and Johnson, *The Origins of Feasts* 171–95, and Martimort et al., *The Liturgy and Time*, 108–29.

16. A great Eastern Orthodox-oriented family devotional that emphasizes the feast days in their tradition and includes ideas for celebrating is Wigglesworth, *Celebrating the Twelve Days of Christmas*.

naming of Jesus. It fits the narrative arc of the story and is a tangible way of marking the chronology of the 12-day season. The Roman Church has instead decided to hold the circumcision and naming on January 3. The Eastern Orthodox church, in line with Anglicans, Lutherans, and others, celebrates the day on January 1st, and commemorates Mary as the Mother of God on December 26, instead of being St. Stephen's Day. In my mind, the branches of the church would do well to commune together and agree on what the best chronology of the 12 days is, for instance, universally making the 26th Stephen's Day, January 1st the circumcision and naming, and then choosing another day, perhaps January 3rd, for Mary as Mother of God. Rather than be bound to the perceived unwavering restrictions of our traditions, for the sake of some semblance of church unity it seems it would be for the benefit of all if there were compromises and adaptations throughout in an attempt to streamline the calendar on the major feast days and seasons. At the same time, we could certainly give each other freedom for variations of our lesser and more idiosyncratic feast days. But for a season as prominent as Christmas, uniformity would be a benefit and aide to the worldwide church, both in how the holiday functions but also in our witness to those outside the church.

The other factor that makes saints' days difficult to incorporate into our traditions is that we simply lack a personal connection to them. While it might be somewhat easier to get people excited to devoting themselves to a saint when they are found in Scripture, as with St. Stephen and St. John, or when it is their congregational namesake, as in a church named "St. Stephen's," we may find it difficult to muster any enthusiasm for the more obscure saints of the 12 days of Christmas, let alone the yearly calendar. During Christmas this would include St. Thomas Beckett, St. Sylvester, St. Basil and St. Gregory Nazianzen, St. Elizabeth Ann Seton, St. John Neumann, John Wyclif, Seraphim Monk of Sarov, and Vendanayagam Samuel Azariah (bishop in India). Though it may reveal more about our communal disparity of church history education, I can imagine many people replied "Who?" to most everyone on that list. But even if you and your community did happen to have a particular devotion to one of those relatively minor saints, you would nonetheless struggle to make obvious connections between them and the ongoing Christmas narrative you are trying to outline during the 12 days. All of the various saints contain a wealth of stories and teachings unto themselves and are worthy of your self-education and devotion, and yet I venture to say you may find it all a bit tedious and abstract trying to explain to children and the average churchgoer why you are devoting so many of the 12 days to different figures of the church throughout history. I can imagine a number of Protestant or nondenominational churches opting out of celebrating *any* of the saints' days, even Stephen and John, and instead choosing to focus only on the days that relate directly to the Christmas narrative.

The role any particular saint will play in the life of a community will always depend on personal affinity, that is, how much a saint comes to mean to you. Due to influences in my own life, I have always been drawn to St. Francis, St. Patrick, St. Benedict, and St. Augustine, but also other figures from my faith heritage, including Thomas Cranmer, John and Charles Wesley, and more modern figures like C. S. Lewis and Rich Mullins. I am drawn to their lives and teachings because of how much they have influenced me personally. Saints Thomas Beckett and Sylvester? At the moment they do not mean a whole lot to me, but that does not mean I will not seek out their lives and learn from them at some point in the future. Personally, I am not sure they will ever find their way into my Christmas traditions though. Which is to say that churches and families will have to discern for themselves how much emphasis they put on the saints and to what extent they want to specifically relate their lives to the 12 days of Christmas.

"Here We Come a-Caroling/Wassailing/Belsnicking/ Mumming/Parading"

There have been two much maligned instances within history when Christmas was banned in certain societies, namely for twelve years during England's Puritan Commonwealth in the middle of the seventeenth century and then later on in the same century in the Massachusetts Bay Colony.[17] These prohibitions of Christmas are significant because they occurred within decidedly Christian cultures. While those of us in the pro-Christmas camp may look back on these puritanical eras with derision, it is nonetheless worth considering why they so adamantly sought to enact laws against the holiday. For, if we found ourselves living in their time and context we very likely would have banned Christmas too, or at least made significant changes to it.

What if Christmas were not simply a sentimental time to gather with family and devote ourselves to worshipping our Savior, but also a "wanton

17. Golby and Purdue, *The Making of the Modern Christmas*, 33–35.

Bacchanalian feast"[18] of unhinged revelry, of riotous parading in the streets by masked and costumed "callithumpian bands"[19] who vandalized and destroyed property, when good citizens were harassed in their homes and made to give over their money and possibly have their sleep intentionally disturbed with raucous noise in the middle of the night? And what if all this unhinged partying, mostly by the young people in your community, resulted in unplanned and underage pregnancies, with newborn babies coming nine months later?[20] Throughout the history of Christmas there is a set of traditions that many people more closely associate with Carnival or Mardi Gras, which, like those festivals, seem to act as a kind of temporary societal pressure valve, relieving one's daily burdens of being overworked and underpaid. For at least one season of the year the lowly can overturn the tables of power on the mighty. In this way, the rowdy rituals hinted at above also mirror the St. Stephen's and Boxing Day begging that came to be associated with the 26th.

These are what I would call group procession rituals and they took on many different names: wassailing, mumming, belsnickling, Parrandas, Reisados, *Mari Lwyd*, Klöpfelnächte, but also the more familiar practices of caroling and parading. With roots going back to the pre-Christian rituals of the Roman Empire and other European countries,[21] the processions contained diverse regional variations, but they all shared a few basic components. This would include a group processing about their neighborhood or town, offering a performance along the way, with the possible expectation they they would receive or themselves give out a reward or some form of hospitality. These processions could take place at any time during Advent on up to the start of Lent. Some regions limited them to specific days, such as only on St. Nicholas's Day, but other regions had multiple instances throughout the season where they would get their group together and go about their neighborhood. In some places groups would go about for successive days during the 12 days and no one would quite know when they might show up at their house. As mentioned above, at times people pushed the boundaries of their society with their processions, actively seeking to disrupt and harass others, while most of the time the processions were expected and enjoyed. For the latter scenario this meant that

18. Golby and Purdue, *The Making of the Modern Christmas*, 35.

19. Nissenbaum, *The Battle for Christmas*, 54.

20. Nissenbaum, *The Battle for Christmas*, 22.

21. Miles, *Christmas Customs and Traditions*, 168–69.

while a community's night might be disrupted, it was acceptable because most people had made a little unhinged rowdiness part of their tradition. Looking in reverse, we can see that the reason behind our more regulated and organized contemporary practice of community parades or the more benevolent practice of caroling from house to house is that the original traditions were so disruptive and potentially harmful. With parades people are allowed to let loose and perform but within an agreed upon route and time period, and with caroling a group can offer their songs to whoever might listen but then decide to politely move on.

For the sake of offering more context, here is a further description of the general ritual along with a few regional variations. Depending on how established the tradition was in a given region, oftentimes it was the group itself who would decide when and where they would go out caroling/wassailing/belsnickling/mumming/parading, whereas at later times a community would agree together when and where processions would occur. Thus we find in some countries processions going out on any night during the 12 days, but in other countries a single day is established, such as Christmas Eve, St. Stephen's, New Year's Eve, or Twelfth Night. Many of the groups dressed up in costumes as one of the Christmas visitors, such as Nicholas, Krampus, or Knecht Ruprecht, as masked animals such as the *Mari Lwyd* horse, or dressed as the opposite sex. Going from house to house and knocking on doors, they would ask the children of the house, and perhaps the adults, to answer a riddle or recite a poem or song with them, and then inquire whether they had been "naughty or nice" that year. Often it was expected that if someone got the riddle wrong or was unable to recite the poem, they would have to give up some money or offer a reward to the group (or be menacingly stuffed into a bag, as mentioned in the previous chapter).

One kind of procession is known as a mummers' play, where, instead of caroling or asking riddles, the group performs a brief comedic and melodramatic skit for the household. Though the plays would vary from place to place, they would typically feature archetypal characters such as Father Christmas, a hero named George (coming in the form of a saint, a knight, or a king), a villain, a damsel in distress, a fool (or ass), and a doctor. Their plots usually included a mock combat accompanied by "a quarrel, a death, and a miraculous restoration to life."[22] The act of putting on the play is called "mumming." In most instances refreshments were expected

22. Bowler, *Encyclopedia of Christmas*, 150, 299, 300.

as a kind of "tip" to the traveling band: ale, cider, mulled wine, cakes, pies, pastries, meats, and cheeses were offered up in this Christmas version of trick or treating. It became common in some places for the bands of revelers to levy curses and ill-wishes back at their hosts if they were denied a gift.[23] However, the most edifying and commonly practiced version of this tradition would typically feature a toast or blessing upon the host family by the travelers, such as this classic example from a 1977 BBC holiday special: "God bless Missus and Master and all the family. Wishing you a merry Christmas and a bright and prosperous New Year; and many of 'em."[24]

Where the practice truly got out of hand was when the band would choose for itself how it would go from house to house, thus venturing into neighborhoods who had not approved of their visits and arriving at any hour of the night or any day during the season. As the bands were often organized by people in the poor working classes, some groups went into wealthy neighborhoods, harassing the people there with threats and violence until they gave up enough money to meet the crowd's satisfaction. Other times the group rage was oriented toward ethnic minorities, or it was gendered, with men acting out toward women.[25] We might imagine these demonstrations as nascent forms of labor unions where the working classes lashed out at those in power. Since they had not yet found a way to reform the entire unjust system of employment under which they were working, they instead futilely attempted to put the powerful in their places by extracting a little more money from them.[26] But through these processions the homeostasis between the wealthy and the poor was never severely altered and the withholding rich never received a full or lasting comeuppance. As a response to these ongoing class battles, many places banned their annual processions altogether, and other places transformed them into something more regulated. Philadelphia's New Year's Mummers Parade is an example of the latter, a beloved annual tradition that transformed the city's violent chaos of the nineteenth century into one of the most extravagantly costumed parades in the the United States[27]

23. Bowler, *Encyclopedia of Christmas*, 20.

24. Keyte, *The New Oxford Book of Carols*, 542.

25. Nissenbaum, *The Battle for Christmas*, 54–55.

26. Davis, "'Making Night Hideous,'" 192.

27. Davis, "'Making Night Hideous,'" 192. In her article Davis details Philadelphia's progression in the nineteenth century on into modern times from banning and being disgusted by these Christmas rituals to adapting them into more acceptable and eventually beloved traditions for their city.

These processions seem somehow linked to the St. Stephen's Day tradition of breaking open the boxes to disperse what others have given to the needy among us. While many of the processions were done in the spirit of jovial goodwill, there is something boldly confrontational about people being desperate enough to stand out on the streets declaring they do not have enough money to survive on. Perhaps, the church can more decisively and proactively meet the needs of our world in such a way where harassing the rich will not be necessary. And, despite this tradition's more unruly manifestations, I believe, as I set out in chapter 6, it can still be a fun and meaningful communal practice, able to be adapted to our contemporary contexts. Finally, please note that I go into more of the Bacchanalian and social inversion traditions in chapter 9.

"It's Not Christmas Until Everyone Gets Their Beating!"

It is worth including a "strange traditions" section in each chapter of this book if only so I can chronicle the practices that are not just archaic oddities but also traditions we today find truly appalling. At the top of this list must surely be the many variations of annual Christmas beatings, most of which were handed out to the unfortunate children of the world, who, depending on local custom, might receive a good thrashing anywhere from December 24 to 28. This tradition was linked to either: one of the gift-bringers who, during their visit, would chastise disobedient and churlish children; or as a consequence for failing to complete their community's agreed upon annual holiday task, such as not knowing their catechism, not knowing an assigned Scripture verse, not being able to answer a riddle, or not getting out of bed in time.[28] The weapons of choice were ashy bundles of sticks, birch rods, whips of holly, and sometimes people made the more brutal choice of using their fists or the backs of their hands.[29] In truth, most beatings were light-hearted (and handed) and were meant to instill health in the recipient as a kind of purging of bad influences and evil spirits.[30] Though in some instances, as in the "Holming" tradition of Wales, young men would go about in the streets armed with holly branches, and, as a form of teasing, would beat any young woman they came across in hopes of drawing blood

28. Bowler, *Encyclopedia of Christmas*, 19; and Miles, *Christmas Customs and Traditions*, 219, 231.

29. Miles, *Christmas Customs and Traditions*, 231.

30. Miles, *Christmas Customs and Traditions*, 207, 317.

with the sharp leaves.[31] Today, hardly any countries persist in keeping their beating traditions alive, and it may surprise many modern people that at one time the practice, whether in jest, in competition, or in cruelty, was actually quite common.

IDEAS FOR CELEBRATING

Isn't There a Better Way to Serve Others at Christmas?

There are legitimate arguments to be made that December 26 should be a day of leisure. After the Christmas preparation and busyness, both familial and ecclesial, it makes sense for the second day of the holiday to have no agendas and to be a time to unwind. Actually, it could be argued the entire 12 days should be a midwinter jubilee where we purposefully rest from work. While I believe there is a kind of seventh day of creation sabbathing, and a new heavens and new earth proclamation in making the season a time of rest, the life of Stephen places before us the challenge to address and embrace the hardships of people most in need in our world. The idea of the St. Stephen's Day "box" that is not opened until after Christmas is unfortunate, as it implies those who "have" have been withholding from the "have nots" during the majority of the year. If the church were listening to and had eyes to see the needs of the world, and if those most blessed with worldly resources were also the most generous and decided to live most humbly, might the concept of breaking open the "box" become obsolete, so to speak?

Which is to say, something about the "traditional" forms of giving to those in need on St. Stephen's Day and throughout the Christmas season should not sit well with us. As followers of Christ, we should not relegate generosity and life-saving help to the world's most vulnerable people for one day or season a year, but instead live as those who, out of a self-giving love, willingly give of our time, resources, and affections. We are to forever be discerning the will of God as we figure out what it means to be these "living sacrifices" offering up our "spiritual worship" as Paul describes in Romans 12. And we do not want to risk Jesus having to rewrite his vision of the Final Judgment, saying "And I came to you naked and hungry, but you turned me away saying 'It is not Christmas, nor is it especially St. Stephen's Day . . .'" In other words, there is an aspect to Christmas giving where we

31. Bowler, *Encyclopedia of Christmas*, 19, 106.

begin to feel like hypocrites, because, even if we help out at a soup kitchen or donate canned goods to a charity, we end up feeling conflicted within ourselves, asking the question "It's good that we're helping people . . . but shouldn't we be helping those in need *all* the time, and not just at Christmas?" Because really, how arrogant are we to think that reserving good deeds for Christmas time means we are actually doing the long-term work of the kingdom? The challenging question to ask is how might we, being rooted in the self-emptying abundance of God's love and provision, continually live so we have just enough for ourselves in order to be able to generously give to people in need?

The two biggest recommendations I can give us are to act both locally (and highly personal) *and* corporately (and thus highly *im*personal) in our giving. The key to local giving is to build long-term relationships with people and organizations in the communities within which you actually live to such an extent that it simply would not make sense to only give at one time during the year. Instead, by seeking to know the people around you who are most in need, you will learn how to be in tune with a local organization's yearly needs. This will enable you to know how to best serve them with monetary gifts, donations, and serving them with your time. My own congregation has begun a relationship with Phoenix Community Development Services, an agency working to help end poverty in our city of Peoria, Illinois, by providing long-term housing and skills training for homeless people.[32] As a church community we have participated in donating specific household and hygienic items that the agency has requested for their tenants and we have participated in a community cleanup and landscaping day. As we move forward, I believe the greater challenge we have is to build lasting relationships with the tenants in the agency's apartment buildings (one of which is right next door to where we worship) and to discover through the messiness of ministry how to serve people in life situations significantly different from our own. This kind of mission would be impossible to make any impact with if we only did a once-a-year donation drive.

Another local and personal approach for giving is for us to simply be aware of the needs of those within our closest geographical and relational proximity and then find a way to serve, love, and disciple them. I know of one Anglican ministry family (the husband is a priest and the wife a deacon), who opens up their home on December 24 for anyone to stop by if

---

32. For more information, please visit their website at https://phoenixcds.org/.

they need some food or would simply benefit by spending time with other people. This kind of practice could be extended as your family's tradition throughout the 12 days. Through years of persistence you could send the message to people around you that your home is a safe haven of hospitality, warmth, and companionship. Many of us will spend the 12 days watching our favorite films, enjoying a televised sporting event, and playing any number of party games. These "secular" activities are the perfect times to invite those we know of who may not have family or friends to spend time with during the season.

It is worth acknowledging that celebrating Christmas, along with participating in other "normal" activities of the season, can be either quite difficult or quite unappealing depending on a person's stage or position in life and what memories they associate with the holiday. It is up to us to be aware of who might be the most in need within our social circles and then be bold enough to take steps to invite those people into our Christmas activities as well as the rest of our lives. The elderly or those who suffer from chronic illnesses have a difficult time getting out of their homes and often times fall out of touch with their faith community. Doing things out in public simply takes too much effort, truly endangers them, or is too embarrassing for them to continually make the effort to overcome the social stigmas they face. How might we find ways to bring church and Christmas celebrations to *them*, to serve them by getting groceries and gifts for their loved ones, and to creatively give them places of honor by making them an integral part of our celebrations? Along these lines, it is worth considering how you might develop relationships with nursing homes, retirement communities, group homes, and hospitals to figure out how to serve their needs during the holidays but also throughout the year. Other groups that may struggle with the season are single people, nonreligious people, people with broken or abusive family relationships, and people who carry significant hurt from churches in their past. Single people often feel like they have no place within many family-centric church cultures. Although Christmas is often a family-centered holiday, and thus intimate by nature, the servant-hearted nature of St. Stephen's Day challenges us to rethink our conception of "family" and to instead consider the larger vision of what the "family of God" looks like. Doing so will challenge us to look around and see who we need to extend grace toward and take a risk by inviting into our homes. How might we invite them into everyday activities such as meals, housework, and yes, our holidays? We also need to be aware that here are the people in our lives who may not be able to muster the strength to enter a church anytime soon, or those who only feel pain when they think of their family. In what ways can we invite them into our lives in the hope of one day reshaping their experience of family and church?

Moving on from the exclusively personal ways we can give of ourselves, one way we can truly be fruitful in our giving, and not need to feel guilty about it, is to go full-on *im*personal and give to a large corporate charity organization that we know is doing good work in the world. While "donating to charity" should never let us off the hook from the personal kinds of ministry mentioned above, it has proven to be much more efficient and beneficial to those most in need to give directly to the organizations who know how to best utilize the money given to them. Instead of putting on a canned food drive, our money can be used by an experienced charity to purchase larger quantities of food that are also fresher and more nutritious. As mentioned in the previous chapter you can go to various charity comparison websites to discern which organizations are run the most effectively, do the most good, or are working toward the cause you are most passionate about.[33] There are some organizations who are learning it serves the greatest need to put money directly into the hands of the poor, such as Give Directly (www.givedirectly.org).

Whatever action your community decides to take regarding "charity" and service work, if you have any notions whatsoever of seeing lasting societal change or of avoiding the "compassion fatigue" that is so prevalent with people who give of their time and resources for a season but ultimately get frustrated or burnt out, the advice of poverty experts is to take as relational and holistic an approach as possible. As laid out in excellent resources such as *When Helping Hurts* and *Toxic Charity*, our goal can never be to simply give people material possessions, as that never addresses the complex systemic and personal reasons people find themselves in poverty to begin with. Using the Gospel as their foundation, these books argue that "Jesus is bringing reconciliation to every last speck of the universe, including both our foundational relationships and the systems that emanate from them. *Poverty is rooted in broken relationships, so the solution to poverty is rooted in the power of Jesus' death and resurrection to put all things into*

33. The information in this paragraph was inspired by the episode "Adam Ruins Giving" from the TV show *Adam Ruins Everything*, directed by Paul Briganti; the article by Matthew Yglesias, "Can the Cans"; and the TED talk video by Joy Sun, "Should You Donate Differently?"

right relationship again."[34] Our approach to poverty as followers of Christ is to seek "to restore people to a full expression of humanness, to being what God created us all to be, people who glorify God by living in right relationship with God, with self, with others, and with the rest of creation.[35] To use an example from *When Helping Hurts*, it does not alleviate a people's "poverty of being" to only go to your city's government housing complex once a year to hand out pre-wrapped Christmas presents for the children there.[36] This ultimately creates shame and inadequacy for the parents there who are not able to provide gifts for their children *themselves.* The challenge of the bigger picture "involves the much harder task of empowering people to *earn* sufficient material things through their own labor, for in doing so we move people closer to being what God created them to be," and can in fact help us all to realize that our work is itself "an act of worship" toward God.[37] Pulling back even further, this approach will cause the church to have to address the larger brokenness and abuses in the systems that have shaped the people in poverty who live next to us in our cities and towns. To sum up, all of these realizations help us see the glaring inadequacy of hit-and-run Christmas charity, and instead confront us to be a people always looking to restore in Jesus's name the full humanity of our neighbors and the whole world.

But, as mentioned above, the other challenge (and indeed appealing draw) of the 12 days is to make it a season of restful leisure, which seems to contradict the effort involved in the call to serve others. What if, however, the postures of leisure and service were combined? What if, as part of our 12-days practices, so far as it is possible, we closed up our shops and factories and stopped working? What if we began taking that time off to be with family, or at least larger sections of that time than in the past? And then, along with significant amounts of rest, what if we also made it a point to have decidedly open homes? What if we brought back the "drop in" for ourselves and others? And what if we had booked so much time for sabbathing during the season that out of our rest a significant amount of our holiday was spent serving and opening up our selves and homes to those in need? Can we imagine what it might look like for the global church to spend the 12-day holiday that way?

34. Corbett and Fikkert, *When Helping Hurts*, 73.
35. Corbett and Fikkert, *When Helping Hurts*, 74.
36. Corbett and Fikkert, *When Helping Hurts*, 61, 62–64.
37. Corbett and Fikkert, *When Helping Hurts*, 74.

Miscellaneous Suggestions

- One way your family can continue to make Boxing Day focused on giving to others is for you to have your own giving box set up next to the tree, or a centralized, high-traffic location in your home. Throughout the whole year or only during Advent you can collect money and loose change to put into the box, and then on the 26th you can open it, take it to the bank, and then get a check ready to send to the charity of your choosing.[38] And if you are so bold (assuming you have some oversight and approval), you can even go around your neighborhood, church, or school and encourage others to get in on the giving as well.

- According to *The Book of Christmas*, one long-held tradition associated with St. Stephen's Day, most likely originating from a monastic community but finding popularity within British schools, was for students to write out the story of some saint or Scripture passage using their best penmanship and then for the most excellent examples to be displayed in a prominent place in the school or church.[39] Obvious seasonal examples would be to copy the nativity and incarnation texts from Matthew, Luke, or John, a passage about Stephen or John from Acts, or anything related to the Christmas saints and feast days. Students could compete for the most excellent version of the same section, or a single class could write out an entire passage, with each student taking a small section of the passage. The writing could be in whatever style the teacher requires, from the standard cursive they are already learning, to a more ornamented calligraphy, to even an illuminated manuscript in the style of the *Book of Kells*. Since this would be a new tradition, unfamiliar to most people, it might make the most thematic sense to begin incorporating it on St. John's Day (December 27), emphasizing the beauty of the written word on a day when the book written by that particular saint centers on the Word made flesh. Even so, you can begin the practice at other times as well, such as in a school before breaking for Christmas vacation, in a children's class at church on the Sundays around the 25th, or as a craft at a Christmas VBS (which I describe in chapter 7).

---

38. Chaney, *The Twelve Days of Christmas*, "St. Stephen's Day."
39. Hervey, *The Book of Christmas*, 310.

- As mentioned at the beginning of this chapter, in some cultures horses have taken on a prominent role for St. Stephen's Day. For those who love horses, horse culture, or if you come from cultures who do, it may be worth it to look into what kinds of traditional blessings, foods, races, and other fun events you can plan for your horses on St. Stephen's Day (though I believe it is difficult to make an actual correlation to how these practices relate to the saint himself.) The same can be said for the various "Wren's Day" activities on the 26th. You may desire to look into reinstating these traditions, as some Irish towns have done, though again the practices surrounding the hunting, killing, and parading of the wren have far stronger pre-Christian roots than any connection to St. Stephen and the coming of Christ.

- St. Stephen's and Boxing Day has also been a time to let loose and be silly. As horses were used to join in on the chase, fox hunts used to be a popular St. Stephen's tradition in England before the practice was banned in 2005. Even so, as way of keeping the traditions alive, in recent years some have taken to going on mock fox hunts with their horses where no actual foxes are chased and killed. Other people have engaged in some St. Stephen's fun by doing a Polar Bear Plunge in a nearly frozen body of water on the 26th—a practice which is also popular on New Year's Day. Finally, many in England look forward to the annual St. Stephen's pantomime plays, which feature playful retellings of many classic fairytales and allow people the opportunity to dress up in ornate costumes and give over-the-top performances.

6

Day 3: Feast of St. John the Evangelist
(December 27)

History and Meaning

Even before December 25 solidified as the date of Christ's birth in the Christian world, different church communities began to group the feast days of the most prominent apostles and early martyrs together at the end of December. Three early church calendars—the Calendar of Nicomedia from circa 363,[1] the Armenian Lectionary dating from the first half of the fifth century and reflecting the earlier customs of the Jerusalem church, and a pieced-together late-fourth-century calendar from Cappadocia—list

---

1. Martimort et al., *The Liturgy and Time*, 120.

with some variation December 26 for Stephen, the 27th for John and James, and the 28th for Peter and Paul.[2] While, as I mention in chapter 7, there are ways to thematically link Stephen, John, and the innocents to Christ's birth, the early church sought to commemorate the revered apostles, evangelists, and martyrs in a cluster of dates right as December was concluding.

In Western churches December 27, the third day of Christmas, solidified into the Feast of St. John, the evangelist and apostle. The authorship of the Gospel of John, the epistles of 1, 2, and 3 John, and Revelation continues to be disputed as either coming from a single source, a composite of authors from what has come to be known as the Johannine community, or separate authors altogether.[3] Though the Gospel of John does not make it absolutely explicit, church history has traditionally determined that the author of the book, noted in 21:24 as "the disciple whom Jesus loved" (and five other passages in the Gospel), is John, one of the original twelve apostles, known, along with Peter and James, for his closeness with Jesus. That disciple was there with Jesus on the mountain during the transfiguration (Luke 9:28–36), and on the cross Jesus declared the disciple to be his mother Mary's son, with Mary now the disciple's mother, where afterwards he took care of her in his home (John 19:26–27).

Particularly in relation to Christ's birth, St. John's Day can be a time to read aloud, meditate on, and have times of worship and prayer centered around the first chapter of the Gospel of John. John's Gospel gives us the "theological" version of the infancy narrative, where we are presented with the challenge and beautiful mystery of the incarnation, that is, the revelation of the Word becoming flesh and dwelling among us (more depth is given to this subject in chapter 2). Also, if your church celebrates a second liturgy on Christmas morning, the Gospel traditionally read at that time is from John chapter 1, and the chance for multiple readings of the same passage throughout the season gives us the opportunity to successively contemplate the profound, sublime truth of what it means that eternal divinity became temporal humanity, the Light shining in darkness, bestowing upon us grace and truth as the Lamb of God who takes away the sin of the world.

---

2. Bradshaw and Johnson, *The Origins of Feasts*, 191–93.

3. Perspectives on this debate are vast and ongoing. Some places to begin are Ashton, *Studying John*; Köstenberger, *Encountering John*; and Brown, *The Gospel According to John I–XII*.

There are not many robust St. John's Day traditions that have continued down to the present. Apart from some basic suggestions at the end of the chapter, I will put the majority of my focus on how a variety of 12-days practices, which have come in and out of fashion throughout history, can be incorporated into the relaxed days following the 25th. In doing so, I give you the options possible for striking a balance between an introverted and an extroverted Christmas, which I explain in detail.

STRANGE TRADITIONS

A Blessing of the Spirits

Possibly based on a legend that John had once drunk poison and lived, his feast day came to be associated with bringing wines and ciders into the church to be blessed. There were superstitions attached to the wine, such as believing it offered protection for the coming year, but often this day led to foolish, excessive drinking, especially since some people tried to drink the entire stock on the day it was blessed.[4] There are ways to make this tradition more solemn and sacred, with a family taking the blessed wine, saying their own prayer of blessing over it, and then sharing a cup of it together.[5] Though people may not need any more excuses to down a glass of their favorite alcoholic beverage, and it may not make sense in your church context to pray blessings over your supplies of alcohol, you are certainly welcome to bring back the tradition.

IDEAS FOR CELEBRATING

An Introvert's Christmas

One of the more sobering and honestly frustrating aspects of researching the 12 days has been realizing that there are not specific traditions assigned for each of the individual days. St. John's Day is a great example of this where, even though the day commemorates a significant saint of the

---

4. Miles, *Christmas Customs and Traditions*, 314–15; and Bowler, *Encyclopedia of Christmas*, 122–23.

5. Chaney, *The Twelve Days of Christmas*, "St. John's Day." Another resource for wine blessings can be found on the Catholic Culture website in their article "Christmas: December 27th."

church, no strong traditions have come to be associated with his day. By taking a step back from the myriad of traditions available to us, it becomes clear that, as I have laid out in previous chapters, the choice of *what to do* for Christmas truly is up to us, and that our choices will always fall under the four categories of worship, celebration, service, and leisure, with the possibility of those categories always overlapping, depending on our activity. Therefore, in looking at St. John's Day, the third day of Christmas, I would like us to consider what kinds of leisurely and celebratory activities we might partake of. To be sure, most of these activities are associated with *other* days during the season or thought of as something to do more generally whenever we like during the 12 days. This section will focus on things we can do for fun and rest and will be broken up into two categories, the first with ideas appealing to the introverts among us, and the second with ideas for extroverts. All of these ideas can, of course, be mixed however you like. Please keep in mind the social group parameters I laid out in chapter 4, as every activity takes on different dynamics based on the size of the group involved.

In some ways we might say the prevailing symbol of an introverted Christmas is the yule log. Though the practice and ceremonies surrounding the tradition has in many ways disappeared, along with the magical properties associated with it, the idea of selecting a massive log to burn in our fireplace to give our home warmth and light during the cold and darkness of the season (assuming a northern hemisphere location) may not seem so foreign to us. An adaptation of the tradition, which makes sense for families without a fireplace, is to purchase a massive candle that can be burned throughout the season. Potentially, as according to tradition, families often tried, if possible, to keep the flame burning without extinguishing it for the entire season. The idea is clear: to create an appealing center in our homes around which to gather and feel safe, warm, and cozy. For many of us, the Christmas tree has already become this center, and may be viewed as a kind of perpetual yule log that "burns" but is not consumed, and as a symbol for Christ, the Light of the world, it gives light and joy to the entire household.

After gathering with our community in worship, we now draw back and regather around this household center, this hearth, in order to enter into our Christmas sabbathing. A true introvert's holiday would be almost completely antisocial, and that certainly may be the preferred option for some. Introverts seem to instinctively know how to spend their alone time, whether it be long successions of reading books, working on an artistic project, watching films and TV, or playing video games. Indeed, there are arguments to be made that this is a "traditional" way to engage in the 12-day feast, though adapted for the individual. My suggestions here will be slightly more communal, and I will let the introverts among us communicate to those around them how secluded they want their holiday to be.

To start with, it is typical for people to play games during the holidays. In chapter 9 I list a few traditional Twelfth Night games, but I would argue the tradition to keep is the general playing of games and not any specific game associated with the season. The amount of games and activities available to us in modern times is endless, so feel free to play whatever you and your family enjoy the best, be it board games, card games, roleplaying games, video games, or puzzles.

Reading stories aloud to each other is another tradition worth bringing back. The end of this book features a list of Christmas-themed stories, novels, and reflections out of which you may want to read a new selection each year or create a tradition by reading from the *same* selection each year. Though it can be adapted for any time of the day, it might make the most sense to read a section or chapter each night, such as from Dickens's *A Christmas Carol*, in the half hour before bedtime. Reading aloud helps us to engage in the story together. One adaptation to this practice is to read aloud or act out a play together, with everyone sharing the different roles, such as Shakespeare's *The Winter's Tale*. More ambitious families may even decide to write their own plays and stories to read aloud. One final adaptation of this practice, is for everyone to take turns sharing their favorite family memories, either recalling Christmases past or a recap of the past year. This gives us the chance to relive our past times together and in some way bring back, if only for a moment, loved ones who have died. Many people find it difficult to be vulnerable enough to open up and share their feelings, but a simple way to encourage this practice would be to ask, "Can everyone share one memory from the past year or a favorite Christmas memory you want to reminisce with us about?" Whether your stories illicit laughter or tears, creating a space where your family feels safe to talk about the past can bring about a great deal of emotional and spiritual healing over the years.

While introverts may have no problem going caroling with a group (please see the next section), they may also want to keep their music at home. It is certainly adequate to put on a record or stream our favorite tunes, but I would recommend we be our own music-makers as much as possible. Even if it is only for one night, find a way to print off the music and lyrics to some favorite carols and sing a few of them together. Whether the singing erupts into boisterous laughter or ascends into solemn worship, the practice of making music together is a communal ritual worth bringing back. You can take this practice a step further by getting out your instruments and learning to play the songs on them. For some this might mean clumsily plunking away on the piano for a few days in order to just (barely) learn a few songs, and for other more practiced families, it will mean organizing a full band who can swiftly play through everyone's favorite carols. Whatever your skill level, the idea that we ourselves are the ones making music is the key.

Watching films and TV and going to concerts and performances during the holidays is another worthy tradition that should not be engaged in passively. Though putting on an actual production is a more extroverted activity, as I address in the next section, going to watch a play or pantomime, going to the theater to watch a new film (or the reshowing of a classic), or simply staying home to watch a sentimental favorite can all be a meaningful and relaxing way to spend time with family. But my recommendation would be to allow the stories, themes, and works of art themselves to spark conversations, discussions, and memories about the past.

In many ways, a traditional "introverted" Christmas means simply to do the leisurely things you love, but to perhaps formalize them in ways you would not during regular, working, non-holiday seasons. In other words, it might take more effort and planning to do a family game night, to learn some music, or to read aloud to each other, but doing so might ensure these practices work their way into a typical week during the year as well. We can engage in communal art-making and game-playing to the level that we are comfortable with, but the key is to engage with each other and to make things together, rather than allow ourselves to go into the zoned-out social cruise-control of self-isolation in front of our screens that is so predominant in our time.

An Extrovert's Christmas

Extroverts, however, will most likely want to consider how many of the same practices listed above can be blown up and put into practice on a much larger scale. Regarding game-playing, there are a number of gaming groups and clubs in cities all over the world, and there are many families who love to informally invite a houseful of people over and organize a large gaming session. The potential for creating Christmas gaming traditions is as large as our imaginations. Churches and schools, as mentioned in chapters 8 and 9 could host gaming nights, which would focus on either specific kinds of games or offer a whole range of game-playing opportunities. Gaming clubs could host their own special nights during the 12 days, opening themselves up to the public in ways that do not typically happen at other times of the year.

But the truly "extroverted" tradition worth considering is some adaptation of the processional rituals mentioned in the previous chapter. Caroling/wassailing/belsnickling/mumming/parading might be considered a kind of mobile party that travels to meet people within a designated area, and makes many stops along the way to give a performance and encourage group participation. Within a neighborhood these stops will be at people's homes, but in a more public space these stops will be wherever the most people tend to gather, such as different stores or a town square. The idea is to gather a group of friends and family, travel around the agreed upon area, and put on a performance that interacts with the people you visit along the way. At each stop you will perform the same set of songs or skits, all with the assumption that hospitality will be given to you in the form of drinks, candies, or prizes. Since "mumming" is not currently familiar in many places, you will need to discern if you call your mobile party "caroling," which is a much more familiar word and concept, but then add the dramatic elements of mumming to it, or you can choose to call it "mumming" but then take on the risk of having to establish a new word and concept into people's yearly rituals. Mumming adds the potential for some humorously improvisational moments between you and the people you are visiting, which the more tender act of carol singing may not provide. You can, of course, choose to not do anything resembling mumming and instead do what people conceive of as conventional caroling. I would recommend, though, adding some of the more jovial elements of the tradition and include a riddle with a prize attached, a toast on the house you are visiting, and a token of hospitality. As you begin planning this kind of tradition, you will need to arrange beforehand with those you will be visiting if those processing will bring the hospitality (like paraders who throw out candy to onlookers) or if each stop along the way will provide it.

After forming the group, the first step to consider is whether or not your caroling/mumming/parading will be a surprise to your hosts or if you will arrange beforehand a window of time in which you will arrive. In many countries, surprise parades around a neighborhood or town have been all but forgotten or eliminated as a tradition. You certainly would have the shock-factor in your favor if you chose to randomly go from house to house singing, performing, and having fun. You also might create a whole host of problems for yourselves, depending on how rambunctious your group is and what time of the night you do it at. Remember that throughout history this kind of tradition was outlawed in many places because the troupes became a public nuisance. One modern adaptation of the practice, and one that people typically find endearing (and worth filming and putting on the internet), is to do a "flash mob" where your group discreetly appears in some public space and begins performing. Think of a mall, city square, subway terminal, or any place where lots of people have gathered. While it starts out seeming like a prank (which is in-keeping with the surprise element of the tradition), the benefit of the flash mob is that it ends up blessing the people on the receiving end: they get a nice chuckle or they end up joining in on the fun themselves. Alternatively, when you choose to pre-plan your parade or caroling route, you get the benefit of building expectation for your hosts and establishing your tradition over the course of multiple years. If you choose to do your own neighborhood or apartment building you can select a date and time, let every household know, and then allow them to opt out of being visited or providing refreshments. But think about which time works best for everyone. While earlier times in the day, such as before supper or bed, are more kid and family friendly, many people are already used to staying up late for New Year's and might consider starting an annual mummers parading tradition with you in the late-night hours of December 31st. Finally, you will need to think about whether your procession is a one-time event during the 12 days—which would make the most sense for attempting a new tradition—or if you plan to venture out on multiple occasions throughout the season—which takes a lot of effort and coordination. A procession can be adapted to many contexts, such as going from store to store in a shopping mall, unit to unit in a hospital, to residents in a retirement community, or to sections of a nursing home.

Next you will need to decide what you will perform. You can certainly stay conventional and choose to only sing carols, sacred and secular, possibly providing music and lyric sheets to encourage people to sing along. However, you can add to the fun by quizzing your hosts with some Christmas trivia, asking a riddle, or playing a game of skill such as getting people to sing all the verses of "The 12 Days of Christmas" without making a mistake. A more serious ceremony, which would require you to be in community with the people you are visiting and to send out information beforehand, would be to ask children (and adults!) questions from a catechism or a Bible verse, such as something that relates to the birth of Christ or about his divinity and humanity. If you desire, you could encourage all manner of silliness and invite participants into a competition, such as a feat of strength, a silly task, or a Best Looking Santa, where you come equipped to dress participants in costumes to be judged or you tell them to be dressed when you come. A relatedly silly custom to bring back is something like the mummers play or skit, which would replace or be added to your singing, though you need to discern how much time you can spend at each stop. If you look up a traditional mummer's play you will find it is structured around an argument, a death, and a restoration of the slain character. Alternatively, you can come up with your own script and parody any Christmas-related story with enough cultural cachet that people will recognize it easily, such as Santa and his elves, Rudolph, the Grinch, *A Christmas Carol*, or *It's a Wonderful Life*. Like with caroling, the idea with mumming is to perform the five-to-ten-minute play for each house you stop at in hopes of receiving refreshments, and then as you depart you offer up a toast to the family or group. If your hosts are familiar enough with your play or you are able to conduct them in the moment, you can invite one or more of them to take on an acting role in it. Another variation is to set up the play in a public area with lots of crowd turnover, such as a mall or civic square, and perform it every fifteen minutes or half an hour. One mumming tradition is to elicit money from the crowds, like street performers do in looking for a tip from those passing by. Collecting money to line your own pockets is most likely not an ethically conscientious practice (unless you are running an actual theater troupe that needs funding), but you could easily bring attention to your annual performances by effectively promoting that you give the money to a charity or ministry.

The final two aspects of caroling and mumming needing consideration are refreshments and costuming. With pre-planned house-to-house visits you could easily ask people to have something prepared for you such as snacks and desserts or any of the traditional holiday beverages such as spiced apple cider, mulled wine, beer, or a traditional wassail. However, your troupe could also give out candies or prizes, as happens in organized parades where paraders throw out treats to the crowds. Costumes can range the full spectrum between nothing but gloves, hat, and winter coat to keep warm, to the modernly conventional red and white elf hats, to something truly traditional (though obscure) as found in the belsnickling or *Mari Lwyd* traditions, which could include a variety of identity-concealing animal and fictional character masks. If you are putting on a mummers play, then at least part of your group would be wearing costumes based on the characters they are playing. Again, think of this "extroverted" Christmas as a kind of gigantic, loosely organized community party, where the celebration comes to you or *you* bring it to the people. Also, it should be noted that if you are hosting a group of mummers or carolers, it is common for the party to be ongoing at your house throughout the evening, which means the festivities begin before they arrive and continue after they leave. Although the highlight of the evening may be when the mummers arrive, you can plan your own set of activities while you are waiting.

As mentioned in the previous chapter, parades, Christmas plays (or pantos), and even concerts, which many communities already organize and produce, are essentially more formalized, prearranged, and thus highly controlled versions of mumming and caroling. This is very literally the case with the Philadelphia New Year's Day Mummer's Parade, where the city turned a once-banned tradition into an extravagant display of elaborate floats and costumes. And though not exactly a direct descendant of mumming, the British Pantomime plays contain similarly over-the-top performances with their retellings of classic folk and fairy tales. Both can be equally silly and fun, but mumming and caroling have the benefit of requiring spontaneity and being out in the public, whereas parade and theater performances have the benefit of being in controlled environments and being highly organized. For introverts, both these kinds of events, whether the spontaneous or planned varieties, are all a bit too much and they nearly always prefer a quiet night at home to whatever the raucous extroverts have planned. However, you very possibly might convince an introvert to go out caroling with you, so long as they do not have to plan the whole thing, and conversely it might even be possible to convince an extrovert to spend an evening relegated to your home, so long as they get to do something fun (and make some noise!) like play games, dance, or sing a song together.

It is helpful to admit upfront to people that practices like mumming and the panto have no real connections to the sacred aspects of Christmas. It is here that the pagan roots of our midwinter feasting really begin to show, and some Christians may want to steer clear of these practices altogether. Dressing up and going around to different homes in hopes of causing some good natured ruckus most certainly does not originate in the church, and yet, depending on how it is put into practice, I believe it can be adapted into something fruitful. For what it is worth, I am not sure that festive desserts, like birthday cakes, have their roots in the church either, but hardly anyone decries them as evil. Similarly, there may be some aspects to pantomimes, such as their crossdressing and crass humor, that Christians may not find edifying, and yet most modern followers of Christ, unlike the early church, are not outright denouncers of performed drama itself. To recall a question I posed before, what we need to seriously consider is how the sacred and worshipful rituals of our holiday will be balanced by the secular and fun.

Regarding this balance, here are two aspects of holiday celebrating worth remembering: First, that people inherently seem to desire wanting to be silly, to let loose, and to pretend to be someone they are not. Any community will need to discern for themselves when their revelry is getting out of hand, is dangerous, annoying, or sinful, but we should not disparage our natural human desire for fun. Second, as stewards of the traditions of the past and advocates for what the future should look like, we should attempt to bring back as many forms of communal art-making as possible. We have made the arts too professionalized, allowing the "official" celebrities, actors, singers, artists, and manufactures to do the making for us. Putting on silly skits as in mumming may seem ridiculous and cause dignified adults some embarrassment, but I would like to invite us all to consider how we might bring pageantry, whimsy, and art-making back into our Christmases, no matter how amateurish it all may seem.[6] The point, in this instance, is to make things together, create experiences, and have fun doing so.

Miscellaneous Suggestions

Here are some other ways St. John's Day can specifically be celebrated:

- As John chapter 1 emphasizes that Jesus is the Light of the world, we could begin holding Christmas light decorating competitions or extravagant art installations for the 27th. If we emphasize it right, people might begin to connect the already beloved aspects of the holiday with its deeper theological truths.

---

6. This is in part the premise of the book *It's Great to Suck at Something* by Karen Rinaldi.

- Your church or school could offer an evening discussion or teaching or a "Theology Pub" night at a local establishment with the opportunity to go over some of the more conceptually difficult aspects of the faith as it relates to Christ's birth and John chapter 1, such as how we define what it means that Jesus is both God and human, some of the heady words associated with the topic of his incarnation, and accompanied with the opportunity for people to voice any questions they might have about the subject.

- And do not forget, there is always the opportunity to engage in the blessing of the wines, whether officially in church or more informally in your home!

7

Day 4: Feast of the Holy Innocents
(December 28)

HISTORY AND MEANING

THE EARLIEST RECORD OF the Feast of the Holy Innocents being celebrated by the church comes from the city of Carthage in North Africa in
the year 505.[1] In other places the day was called Childermas or the word
"Infants" was used instead of Innocents.[2] This fourth day of Christmas is
a difficult one to explain to children. In remembrance of the male children from Bethlehem slaughtered by Herod in Matthew 2:16–18, it is an

1. Adam, *The Liturgical Year*, 143.

2. Miles, *Christmas Customs and Traditions*, 315.

odd and troubling holy day of sorrow placed right in the middle of our feasting and celebrating. Adults may be tempted to glaze over the events of this day due to the subject matter, or ignore it altogether, but I see this as unwise. Speaking personally, even though I was troubled as a child in being confronted by the massacre of the young children, I mostly took the story at face value, accepting it for what it was. The story, I believe, served to help me establish the existence of evil in our world, though understood on a child's level. Children are often more resilient and attuned to evil than we give them credit for and are already prepared for stories such as these in their own way.

Placed within Matthew chapter 2, the event is a culmination of the visit of the wise men from the east who came to Jerusalem asking, "Where is he who has been born king of the Jews?" They had seen and tracked this new king's star, and now, having come before Herod, sought to worship him. Matthew says this news was troubling to Herod and all of Jerusalem, and as a means of discovering where this king was to be born he assembled the chief priests and scribes and gleaned from them that the Christ was to be born in Bethlehem, David's city. Herod then calls back the wise men in secret, asks them to go to Bethlehem, find the new king, and come back to Jerusalem to tell him about the king so he too can go worship the child. After finding Jesus and Mary and presenting him with their gifts (which we celebrate on the Feast of Epiphany), the wise men along with Joseph are warned in a dream about Herod, resulting in the men returning to their homeland without honoring Herod's request. Joseph, Mary, and Jesus flee to Egypt, where they remain until after Herod died. Finding himself "tricked by the wise men," Herod in his wrath and fury had all the male children two years and under in Bethlehem and its surrounding region killed. Matthew points us to the fulfilled prophecy of Jeremiah 31:15, of "Rachel weeping for her children; she refused to be comforted, because they are no more." While at certain times in church history the number of the murdered was thought to be as many as 144,000, it is now believed around a dozen children would have lost their lives based on population estimates at the time.[3]

Historically, Herod, though a wealthy ruler known for his building projects and success in military battles,[4] was not popular among his people. He was seen as a puppet king too connected to his Roman overlords and not particularly devoted to the Jewish faith. On top of this, he reacted in

3. Bowler, *Encyclopedia of Christmas*, 143.

4. Beers, *The Savior*, 104–5.

violence to anyone threatening his rule, having had his wife, his brother, his sister's two husbands, and his son executed.[5] In an iconic quote attributed to Augustus Caesar, it was declared "It is better to be Herod's pig than his son," a quip referring to the Jewish law of abstaining from pork.[6]

What we can glean from Matthew and the historical record is that from the start Christ's birth was a political and social disruptor, even while living quietly under the radar for the first years of his life. Christ's heavenly kingship as the divine *Logos*, the Word of God, was to now have jurisdiction on earth, and thus his rule was a threat to earthly kings. In the massacre of the innocents we see a great evil committed out of fear that another ruler—a more fit ruler—may in fact take Herod's place. Herod would have had no comprehension of what kind of kingdom this Christ would have established, but all that mattered was that the Christ's rule would not be *his* rule. Most likely Herod would have only been able to think in the paradigms of other earthly kings such as himself, and thus would have assumed this new king would rise up to dethrone and kill him. As such, he could only think of one, final solution: to stamp out the threat before the threat stamped out him. We can rejoice in God's mercy that this did not happen. And yet the tragedy of lost life remains, even as it is juxtaposed with the ultimate victory of Christ over sin and death.

As the third holy day after Christmas Day, the Feast of the Holy Innocents is a culmination, of sorts, of martyrs for Christ: Stephen (Dec. 26) was the first martyr of the church, having spilled his blood voluntarily and with love, John (Dec. 27) would have voluntarily died out of love but did not end up being executed, and the innocents of the 28th were executed, but not voluntarily so.[7] Augustine viewed the children as "the first buds of the Church killed by the frost of persecution; they died not only for Christ, but in his stead."[8] This feast day is mournful and heavy and in modern times has come to be connected for some with the murder of the unborn through abortion or any tragedy involving the murder and abuse of children. Matthew's story is bound up in the Feast of the Epiphany where the wise men of the east did not act in violence toward Jesus and did not expose him to the corrupt Herod, but instead offered their worship to him. And yet, on this day we can dwell in the suffering of those children who lost their lives. We

---

5. "Holy Innocents," para. 1.

6. Josephus, *Josephus: The Essential Works*, 257.

7. Adam, *The Liturgical Year*, 142.

8. Holweck, "Holy Innocents," para. 5.

can contemplate all those people, both young and old, unwittingly caught up in the unjust violence of rulers, nations, and cruel regulations that have no regard for human life and that seek to destroy and wipe out any threat or anyone who happens to be in their way. As we mourn with those who mourn, we can also rejoice that Christ our King did come not as one wielding the sword and not as one "to be served but to serve, and to give his life as a ransom for many" (Matt 20:28).

STRANGE TRADITIONS

An Unlucky Day, with More Beatings, and a Boy Bishop

In the medieval period the Feast of the Holy Innocents was generally seen as an unlucky day, perhaps because people connected it to the death of children.[9] As a result of this superstition, many places observed it by not working: sailors would not sail, the dead would not be buried, and people would refrain even from washing themselves.[10] In Germany, there was a tradition that on the feast day it was believed the spirits of unbaptized children would go wandering around the world, but if someone saw them and addressed them with a Christian name they would be set free to enter heaven.[11]

Then of course, as established in chapter 5, there were the beatings. Many such whipping customs were associated with Innocents' Day, and the chosen weapons were again tree branches or brooms. One supposed reason for this was an attempt to embed the seriousness and cruelty of Herod's massacre into the minds of children (that its memory "might stick the closer; and, in a moderate proportion, to act over the crueltie [sic] again in kind"[12]), and in some cases to drive away evil spirits. In some places, if a child was whipped, then someone had to offer them tasty food in return for the whipping endured. In other places, children who were caught in bed during the morning of the feast day got a whipping from their parents, while still in others, the children earliest to rise were allowed to beat the children still lazily remaining in bed. These traditions most certainly had

9. Miles, *Christmas Customs and Traditions*, 315.

10. Bowler, *Encyclopedia of Christmas*, 41.

11. Bowler, *Encyclopedia of Christmas*, 114.

12. Miles, *Christmas Customs and Traditions*, 315.

pagan origins, though it must be said the beatings were rarely extreme and instead served as a kind of teasing.[13]

The final oddity arising from Holy Innocents' Day was the custom of the "Boy Bishop." In some places before the Reformation, a choir boy who was elected by his peers on December 6 was to preside as the bishop until December 28. He would process in, wearing the bishop's garments and mitre, carrying his shepherd staff, and even give the sermon, take up the offering, and pray the benediction. Sometimes the bishop's ministers and perhaps the bishop himself were made to take on the menial responsibilities of the incense bearers and acolytes. A few women were also said to celebrate the practice in their nunneries. Though I say more on the subject in chapter 9, we can see in this practice the "social inversion" that was often practiced during the season, as in the Feast of Fools (January 1), the Feast of the Ass (January 14), or on Twelfth Night (January 5). There was a reversal of roles where the low became high, the high became low, and people were allowed to dress up and take on personas entirely foreign to who they truly were. Nonetheless, during the Reformation Henry VIII saw the practice as a sacrilegious mockery of the priestly office and the liturgy, and thus put a stop to it.[14]

Ideas for Celebrating

Christmas Eve through December 27 were days mostly reserved for family and gathered worship, leisurely fun, and service to others, but the Feast of the Holy Innocents can signify a shift in how the 12 days are celebrated as a community. By December 28 both children and parents are starting to get cabin fever. The elation from opening presents (and playing with those presents) has now diminished, Christmas *ennui* sets in where suddenly there is "nothing to do" in the mind of a child, and parents legitimately start wondering, "When does school start back up again? WHY doesn't school start before the New Year? WHO decides these things?!" The solution to this dilemma may be relatively simple: CVBS, that is, a *Christmas* Vacation Bible School, or at least some variation of it, with the option of putting on a Christmas or Epiphany pageant play.

---

13. Miles, *Christmas Customs and Traditions*, 315–17.

14. Miles, *Christmas Customs and Traditions*, 306–8; and Bowler, *Encyclopedia of Christmas*, 28, 85–86.

I will get into the recommended practices in more detail below, but for now I will lay out a few potential options for a CVBS. In essence, the idea is simple enough: starting on December 28, have one or more days of fun and learning for children that resembles in some way the format of a Vacation Bible School. You can tell the story of Christ's birth, have kids act out the story, play games, and enjoy snacks or a meal. Choosing to put on some variation of a VBS can serve both the families of your church community and the families of your community at large, as it is fun for the kids and a relief for parents!

Believe me, there is a tension in this idea: putting on a VBS right after Christmas certainly puts more strain on your children's pastors, workers, and teachers. However, creating an event that people in your town, city, and region *want* to send their kids to in the middle of the winter doldrums could be a way to serve parents and share the Good News of Christ's coming with the broader community. Along with all this, a CVBS gives you the opportunity to demonstrate to families *how* Christmas is a longer festival and how it can be celebrated that way, especially if your community gathered for worship on the 24th and 25th and is looking to gather for more fun as the season comes to a close, either on New Year's or Epiphany. In other words, the best way to inculturate people to the idea of the 12 days of Christmas is to give them tangible and meaningful traditions to look forward to every year. For your consideration, listed here are a few of the options you can consider for a CVBS.

The One-Day Option

Since putting on an entire VBS program may be too much heavy lifting for many churches, simply put on a fun, one-day event. A full-fledged VBS program is not necessary. Parents will be grateful enough for a single morning when they can drop their kids off for a few hours (9:00 a.m.–12:30 p.m., for example, if you include a lunch). The program does not need to be elaborate, but can include a lesson on the story of the Holy Innocents (or the entire story of Herod, the wise men, and the Holy Family's flight to Egypt), an overview of the different feast days of the 12 days, Christmas-themed games, carol singing, and then end with a meal or snack. A slightly more ambitious idea would be to put on an impromptu Christmas pageant play, where the kids play different roles, put on costumes, and are given stage directions from an adult (or older child) narrator. This can obviously be taken a number of directions, but the benefit of the one-day option is that it's relatively easy to fill a few hours with enriching and fun activities, without putting too much strain on the organizers.

The Two- to Three- (or Four!) Day Option

Most summer VBSs run for three to five days. If your church has the resources and organizational capabilities you may want to consider putting on a full-fledged Christmas VBS. VBSs these days can be pretty elaborate, ranging from highly organized lesson plans to highly produced video series supplemented with on-stage performances. I will reserve writing a curriculum for a CVBS for another author, but stretching out your program over a few days gives you the chance to catechize children in the larger Christmas narrative. The story could be broken up into logical sections over the days, beginning with the Advent narrative and ending with the Presentation of Jesus (Luke 2:22–40). Of course some churches may already be going over the Advent, Christmas, and Epiphany narratives in their Sunday school, kids' church, or education hours, but doing so in a concentrated CVBS setting offers the opportunity to be more immersive, tactile, and in-depth in your pedagogical approach.

The benefit of having a longer CVBS is that along with all the other fun activities and lesson times, children can be rehearsing for an actual Christmas pageant play. This can be performed at the end of the final day of CVBS or in the evening of the final day of CVBS. This will give children a larger project to work toward together, as well as provide a culmination of the previous few days. And here, perhaps, is one of the key benefits for having a Christmas Vacation Bible School with an attached Christmas pageant: if yours is the kind of church which likes to put on Christmas pageants, this idea ensures that families and children's workers are not wearing themselves out with long practices *before* Christmas day, but instead *after*. There will be no threat to family time or the necessary busyness in preparation for the build up to Christmas Day, but instead *afterward* when everything slows down and people are looking for something to do.

With all this said, it *is* worth noting that a church could put on a longer CVBS without it having to be *too* ambitious. Having two to three mornings for lessons, singing, learning the story, and playing games can actually be relatively low-key. In this sense, a church staff can certainly choose their level of organization. A highly ambitious, hyped-up production may actually be a hindrance toward kids having fun and learning what they need to learn. Remember, this season is about us walking through the story *to-gether*. If a child walks away from a CVBS having internalized the story, having learned how to pray and praise God with their hearts and minds, and having lots of fun with people they love and who love them, then your CVBS will have been a grand success.

There is a significant problem, however, with having a Christmas pageant that would be held around December 30–31: It's not the Feast of the Epiphany yet and many churches may want to purposefully hold off on re-enacting the wise men portion of the story. Which leads to the final option.

A Longer CVBS That Leads to a Christmas Pageant Performed on the Feast of the Epiphany or Epiphany Sunday

In this option you could have the same longer version of a CVBS that instead culminates in a pageant when your church celebrates Epiphany on January 6 or the closest Sunday to it. Culturally, this would shift people's yearly expectations from having a pageant performed on Christmas Eve or Day (or even in the weeks before Christmas, as many places do), to having it performed on Epiphany, when the full nativity narrative can be reenacted. This also gives you another advantage in teaching children the story: you can depict Jesus's birth and the visiting of the wise men as two events separated by a significant amount of time. It did not all happen in one night, but instead slowly unfolded over the course of a few months or even years, and it is important to give children a sense of this long stretch of time. The visitations of the angel of the Lord to Zechariah, Joseph, and Mary; Elizabeth's and Mary's pregnancies; the naming of John the Baptist; the birth of Jesus; the Herod and wise men story; the circumcision and naming of Jesus; the flight into Egypt; and the presentation of Jesus in the temple could all be part of the pageant play. Of course, if that's too ambitious, a simple retelling of Jesus's birth and the Epiphany would suffice. All of which is to say, there are *options* for performing a Christmas or Epiphany pageant, each of which can present to children the breadth of the nativity story.

One final option for putting on a CVBS and pageant play is to divide up the VBS into two separate days, on December 28 and 31, with a break in between. As you will see in the next chapter, I give congregational suggestions for celebrating New Year's Eve, New Year's, and the Feast of the Holy Name. Depending on your level of ambition, you could put on a CVBS that culminates on the festivities of December 31, including pageant rehearsals every one of those days, or you could simply have two days of celebrating.

In this instance you meet on the 28th for activities and rehearsals, break for a few days, and then meet again on the 31st for some more activities and rehearsals. These would be fun events for children (like a VBS) but would also include a good section of time to rehearse for the pageant. Then, another rehearsal could be had the day before Epiphany or the Saturday before Epiphany Sunday. This would give you three potential rehearsals for the pageant where you would not have to put on an extravagant CVBS program. In this scenario your times of fun and learning would be balanced with the concentrated work of rehearsal time.

What I am hoping that you see in all of this is the spectrum of options at your disposal. A CVBS can be highly produced and organized, it can be fun and educational, or it can be a mixture. In the same way, a pageant play can be a highly scripted and ambitious production involving numerous rehearsals, or it can be done impromptu in the vein of play-acting.

Miscellaneous Suggestions

Now, with the larger picture of CVBS and the pageant presented, let's move on to a list of ideas for how the Feast of the Holy Innocents can be celebrated.[15] As always, please remember anything appropriate for a church community can be adapted for a family, school, or a homeschool co-op:

- Especially if your Feast of the Holy Innocents day is a one-off event for your community, go in-depth with the story of Herod, the wise men, and the massacre. Older children can reenact it for the younger children or a narrator can guide the reenactment in the moment with a prewritten script. Another option would be to find a gifted storyteller or teacher to do an immersive telling of the story.

- Since Innocents' Day is in essence a solemn and somber event, a yearly tradition you can teach families is for children to give up one of their beloved new gifts to give away to someone in need. Obviously, the church would need to develop a system for where gifts can be given and set standards for the kinds of gifts given. And certainly, children could opt out of this gesture, especially if they come from families already in need. At the same time, many of our children come from families with an abundance of possessions, and Christmas is a time where perhaps an overabundance of gifts are given. Seeing the Feast

---

15. Ackerman and Ackerman, *To God Be the Glory*, 151–52.

of the Holy Innocents as a day to give to others in need could make a big impact on the way children see our world and their place in it. By the way, this same practice could be implemented on Epiphany or Epiphany Sunday to coincide with the gifts of the wise men. Either way, giving to those in need and giving up our possessions are important practices to build into children. Remember though, as explained in chapter 5, many families do not want pre-used or hand-me-down toys for their children, as this seemingly kind gesture can actually be demeaning. In other words, it may be worth discerning what giving practices we can instill in our children that do the most good, in both their lives and in the lives of those we are giving to.

- Conversely, and depending on the number of children present, Innocents' Day could be a great time for one of your pastors to give a gift to the children. The gift could vary on the spectrum from a piece of candy all the way to an object with a lesson attached to it that the children can remember the day by.

- Depending on how the day is organized, you can begin or end the time with a meal. Have a pancake breakfast or brunch with eggs, sausage, and bacon, or simply order pizza for lunch.

- In the classrooms or in the hall where the meal will be, each table can be decorated visually with different images from a Christmas carol and those tables could lead the group in their designated carol. In the same way, quiz games could be developed where children have to guess the titles of carols based on certain clues. Any number of Christmas-themed games, for small or large groups, can be looked up or invented.

- You could end the morning with a piñata. This can be a way to teach them about Mexican Christmas traditions. You could get a piñata for the older and younger kids so it's fair. Each child can receive their own bag, with their name on it, and then start collecting candy when the fun begins. Finally, you may want to reserve having a piñata for your New Year's or Epiphany parties and not on Holy Innocents' Day, or you may want to offer multiple opportunities for children to get out some aggression during the 12 days by having piñatas at more than one church event.

-

The motivation for the day (as with any good VBS) should be to seek the right balance between fun, worship, and learning.

8

Day 8: Feast of the Holy Name and Circumcision, New Year's, and Holy Family Sunday (December 31 & January 1)

HISTORY AND MEANING

THE OCTAVE, OR FIRST week, of Christmas culminates with the eighth day of the season on January 1 with the Feast of the Holy Name or the Feast of the Circumcision. In mainstream Western culture it also doubles as New Year's Day, and thus churches may want to take advantage of the correlation and put on events that celebrate both at once. The naming or circumcision of Jesus does seem to have been a prominent feast on the church calendar at some points in history, but it has also been moved around at times, as seen in the Roman Catholic Church's placement of it on January 3. Moving forward, we have an opportunity to shape the Christmas narrative to the extent where even if the day does not become a culturally prominent feast, we can at least help our communities enter into the chronology of Jesus's birth by marking the eighth day of the season with his naming and circumcision. Along these lines, this feast day also helps us reflect on the experience of the Holy Family in the months after Christ's birth as well as how that connects to their Jewish identity and the Mosaic Law they were adhering to.

As it deals with genitalia and pain, especially that of our Savior, Jesus's circumcision may cause a significant amount of embarrassment and awkwardness when brought up in conversation, let alone a day of commemoration, which is why in recent years the naming aspect of the feast has taken on greater significance. Even so, the rite of circumcision was given special emphasis in Scripture and early church writings, and its connection to Christ and the broader faith is worth exploring. Commanded by God to Abraham and his descendants in Genesis 17:9–14 (and also to Moses in Exod 13:1–2 and Lev 12:1–5), circumcising the foreskin of every male child eight days after birth was a sign of God's "everlasting covenant" with his people. Christ's circumcision then was not so much for himself as it was for the redemption of his people: "But when the fullness of time had come, God sent forth his Son, born of woman, *born under the law*, to redeem those who were under the law" (Gal 4:4–5, emphasis mine), and that also "he had to be made like his brothers *in every respect*, so that he might become a merciful and faithful high priest in the service of God" (Heb 2:17, emphasis mine). Circumcision was one of the primary ways that Jesus came under the law and was made to be like his brothers in every respect. But early in the life of the church baptism quickly replaced circumcision as act of redemption and a rite of initiation into God's people: "In him also you were circumcised with a circumcision made without hands, by putting off the body of the flesh, by the circumcision of Christ, having been buried with him in baptism, in which you were also raised with him through faith in the powerful working of God, who raised him from the dead" (Col 2:11–12). In the New Covenant, baptism, not circumcision, is our sign of God's faithfulness and forgiveness, and it applies to both sexes, not only males. Though the Jerusalem council in Acts 15 put forward the definitive statement of placing "no greater burden" upon the church regarding circumcision (Acts 15:28), it has continued to be debated as being either unnecessary or an act of moral and physical necessity, running the gamut from coming back into fashion to being adamantly opposed in various cultures throughout history.

Some theologians assert though that even Luke the Evangelist subordinated Christ's circumcision to his naming in Luke 2:21, ignoring his coming under the Mosaic Law until it related to his presentation at the temple in 2:22–24.[1] Thus his naming was significant based on its relation to the command of the angel Gabriel in Luke 1:31,[2] that he will be called Jesus, "Son of the Most High" and that, as his name indicates, "he will save his people from their sins" (Matt 1:21). Our given names often seem to have prophetic impact for the shape and direction of our lives, and regarding Jesus it is important to pay attention to the times Scripture emphasizes the power and saving grace associated with his name: "And there is salvation in no one else, for there is no other name under heaven given among men by which we must be saved" (Acts 4:12).

Despite this subordination, which we should keep in mind when planning how to focus our celebrations of the feast, thinkers of the church have sought to discern what Christ's circumcision may in fact mean. Many saw the act not just as his obedience to the Law of Moses but also as a first shedding of blood that prefigured his saving death on the cross, and was thus the "beginning of our redemption."[3] Christ, who himself did not need to be purified by either circumcision nor baptism, nonetheless submitted himself to both for our own redemption, that we may no longer need to subject ourselves to circumcision, but instead receive the Good News of redemption in the waters of baptism.[4] St. Bernard linked both Christ's circumcision and naming to his incarnation, emphasizing how he was truly God and truly man in the flesh: "But recognize the mediator between God and humankind who from the very beginning of his birth joins what is human to what is divine, the lowest to the highest . . . Similarly, his circumcision proves the reality of the human nature he has taken on, and the name which is above all names declares the glory of his majesty."[5] We might say he was "circumcised as a true son of Abraham, [but] he is called Jesus as a

---

1. Brown, *The Birth of the Messiah*, 432–33.
2. Brown, *The Birth of the Messiah*, 681.
3. Steinberg, *The Sexuality of Christ in Renaissance Art*, 50, 57–58.
4. Steinberg, *The Sexuality of Christ in Renaissance Art*, 50, 53.
5. Bernard of Clairvaux, *Sermons For Advent*, 140.

true son of God."[6] Finally, though the symbolic meaning of ancient numerology is often lost on us moderns, other thinkers associated circumcision on the eighth day with Christ's resurrection on Sunday, the eighth day of the week and its inauguration of the new creation.[7] Thinkers such as St. Thomas Aquinas, the Venerable Bede, St. Augustine, St. Bonaventure, St. Ambrose, and the medieval work *The Golden Legend* all give their own versions of these thoughts and are worth exploring, as art historian Leo Steinberg expertly summarizes in his book *The Sexuality of Christ in Renaissance Art and in Modern Oblivion.*

The name of Jesus, the significance and meaning of which I mentioned above, is often depicted in what is called a "Christogram." The most recognizable of these is the Chi-Rho, which contains a combination of the Greek letters for X (*chi*) and P (*rho*), the first two letters in Christ's name, and gives the image of a kind of cross. The emperor Constantine is known for making this Christogram famous and having his armies hold it aloft as a symbol of strength and victory in battle. A Christogram more commonly associated with the Feast of the Holy Name is IHS, which consists of the first three letters of Jesus's name in Greek, *iota, eta,* and *sigma.* Artistic renderings of this Christogram often feature a cross and three nails embedded into the letters, the sun (or rays of light) emanating outward in all directions, and angels hailing his majesty.

Though not numerically exact, this feast represents the middle of the 12 days and manages to pair well with Holy Family Sunday, which some churches (most notably Roman Catholics) have taken to celebrating more in recent years, and falls on the Sunday after Christmas Day (unless Christmas is on a Sunday, in which case it is celebrated on December 30). Though the passages find their way into other weeks in the lectionary, the three-year cycle of Gospel readings for Holy Family Sunday include the flight into Egypt, Christ's presentation at the temple, and Mary and Joseph's discovery of the boy Jesus schooling the elders in the temple. The "Christmas" chronology may jump around a bit with Holy Family Sunday, but the day nonetheless offers us an opportunity to look to Christ's earthly family as a model for our own, to learn from their times of crisis as they sought to parent the Son of God, and to also be in awe with just how unique Christ was as an infant and child.[8]

6. Steinberg, *The Sexuality of Christ in Renaissance Art,* 55.

7. Steinberg, *The Sexuality of Christ in Renaissance Art,* 52.

8. Martimort et al., *The Liturgy and Time,* 85.

As a holiday, New Year's has been seen as a time of feasting, house visits, elaborate galas and soirées, and at certain times throughout history the holiday when the largest gifts are given to family and friends.[9] Many of these same traditions are even found in the New Year's practices of non-Western cultures who celebrate it at a different time of the year. The desire to "party hard" at New Year's can be seen as a kind of thanksgiving for (and reveling in) the abundance of the year that is past as well as a hope that abundance continues in the year to come.[10] Even so, bittersweet melancholy is embedded into the nature of the holiday, as symbolized in the Roman god Janus, who is always depicted as having two combined heads, one looking into the past and one into the future. These two heads symbolize change and the passage of time, new beginnings and the fading away of old things that yet still linger with us, and our venturing through the many doorways and gateways of our lives, both literal and figural.[11] New Year's, as demonstrated through people's perpetual desire to make "resolutions" for the coming year, seems to be bound up in the tension between our desire to make changes and better ourselves on one hand and the circumstances of life we are unable to change due our human frailties on the other hand. The transition into the new year affords us the opportunity to reflect on our possible areas of growth, express gratitude to God for the victories of the past, lament and rejoice over our loved ones who have died, and ponder with humility the areas of our lives where we have *not* seen victory.

And so when we raise our glass high and propose a toast, we know it is a drink mixed with joy and sadness and we partake of that drink together. The New Year is yet another time that communities have traditionally gone on processions to each other's houses, and we can see within customary carols such as "Auld Lang Syne," "Here We Come a-Wassailing" (or Caroling), "Wassail! Wassail All over the Town," and "Deck the Halls" a desire to offer a blessing and raise a toast to everyone we meet for the year to come. Our desire to let loose is a mutual acknowledgement that life is hard and our singing and toasting of each other demonstrates a desire to see God's blessing come to the lives of those we live in community with.

After delving into some strange (and potentially off-putting) New Year's traditions, this chapter gives suggestions for what our partying can

---

9. Miles, *Christmas Customs and Traditions*, 322.

10. Miles, *Christmas Customs and Traditions*, 321.

11. Hervey, *The Book of Christmas*, 320.

look like, how we can incorporate sacred aspects into it, and how the concept of resolutions can be approached in a new way.

STRANGE TRADITIONS

Don't Start the Year Off on the Wrong Foot!

One relatively prominent New Year's tradition that has thankfully fallen out of fashion in most countries is the practice of "firstfooting." Though perhaps best known as a Scottish or British Isles tradition (where it is still popular), the superstitious custom took root in many countries as well. The basic premise is that it truly matters which foot is the first to cross the threshold of your home after the new year has come, and it is good luck to have the right person as your "firstfoot" and bad luck to have the "wrong" person. People would apparently go so far as to pre-arrange their firstfooting visit, in order to ensure good fortune for the coming year. The approved visitors ranged from the innocently sweet—young mistresses awaited the firstfooting of their requited love[12]—while others simply preferred a bachelor, their own grandchildren, or hired servants.[13] The list of undesirable visitors are immediately offensive to modern sensibilities—women were considered the most unlucky firstfooters, but in some places so were blond or red haired people in favor of dark haired people.[14] Women may have been deemed unwanted firstfooters due to the "curse of Eve" and being considered the "inferior sex," but dark haired people seem to be preferred because fair haired people were associated with the invading conquerors to Britain.[15] The tradition varied from region to region though, with some places actually *desiring* fair haired people, to other places rejecting people who were flatfooted or unibrowed, to still other places desiring above all a "footling," that is, a man who had been born feet first.[16] All of this is evidence that superstitions are quite often bizarre and inexplicable, as well as cruelly prejudiced. Though no longer a part of most people's New Year's celebrations, firstfooting points to how much fearful and prejudiced superstitions easily embedded themselves into people's regular customs.

12. Hervey, *The Book of Christmas*, 320.
13. Miles, *Christmas Customs and Traditions*, 325.
14. Miles, *Christmas Customs and Traditions*, 324–25.
15. Miles, *Christmas Customs and Traditions*, 326.
16. Bowler, *Encyclopedia of Christmas*, 84.

A Most (W)holy Awkward Relic
(That We Thankfully Cannot Find)

Although the relics of the saints have been much sought after throughout Christian history for their ability to bestow restorative healing and supernatural grace to the faithful who pilgrimage to their lauded resting places, no relic could be more peculiar or a cause for queasiness (while still undeniably holy!) than that of Christ's circumcised foreskin. Although, as mentioned above, thinkers of old have pondered the theological depths regarding the meaning of Christ's circumcision, it is nonetheless astounding to think that at times people thought they had found his foreskin and then boldly displayed it in some manner for the sake of veneration and devotion. While the ancient and modern history of this supposed relic is documented in full in David Farley's book *An Irreverent Curiosity*, the essentials are that in the year 800 the foreskin was reputedly given to the Emperor Charlemagne by an angel, who then gave it to Pope Leo III.[17] Over the centuries a slew of cities claimed they had the authentic foreskin, including "Akin, Antwerp, Heldesheim, Besancon, Calcata, and Rome,"[18] on up to eighteen total cities during the Middle Ages.[19] Eventually, the town and monastery of Calcata, Italy became the most prominent location for the relic, where it was put on display every year on the January 1 feast day. Otherwise it was "kept behind bronze doors over the altar in the Church of the Most Holy Name of Jesus" until, that is, it was reported lost in 1983.[20] Thankfully the Catholic Church now discourages its members from emphasizing it or even mentioning it, by way of official decrees. Hopefully the whole idea will fall into blushingly quizzical obscurity.

IDEAS FOR CELEBRATING

The Many Ways to Throw a Party

Partying at New Year's can take on many forms. You could venture out and go caroling/mumming/wassailing, as suggested in previous chapters, offering well wishes to your neighbors as you sing a carol, offer a toast, and share

17. Rocca, "Searching for Christianity's Most Sensitive Remnant," para. 8.

18. Foote and Wheeler, *Crimes of Christianity*, 94.

19. Rocca, "Searching for Christianity's most sensitive remnant," para. 9.

20. Rocca, "Searching for Christianity's most sensitive remnant," para. 9.

a glass of a tasty beverage. The Scottish Hogmanay traditions feature their own processional rituals which include people carrying different kinds of portable fire-makers, such as torches and handmade wire fireballs, as well as costumed pageantry similar to the Philadelphia Mummers Parade. While you can certainly partake of the various televised New Year's countdowns, you can also literally ring in the new year with your own set of clanging bells, by setting off fireworks, or by lighting a bonfire as the old year ticks down. Like other times during the 12 days, New Year's Eve and Day can also become a general time for open houses amongst neighbors where drop-ins are welcomed and expected and finger foods and leftovers are readily available. Of course your feasting can be expanded to a larger scale and you can make your own special meat and sweet pies, cakes, breads, pretzels, or any traditional dish according to your custom. Your church or home can become the venue for a game or movie night, and youth groups, much to the chagrin of many parents and youth leaders, can offer all-night lock-ins that deprive young people of sleep while also loading them up on sugary, caffeinated drinks, pizza, and all the goofy fun they can cram into the evening until morning.[21]

A church game night can actually be a relatively low maintenance event, but something more elaborate would be to put on a New Year's costume party or fancy dress ball. There is great appeal for many in putting on a kind of adult prom where people can dress up as much as they like and there is food, music, dancing, and celebratory drinking. If this does not work as a church event in your context, other possible venues could be a banquet center, a local pub with a side room, or even in someone's home. Along these same lines, "masking" and costume dressing has morphed into the modern-day and often elaborate cosplaying, which means dressing as a favorite fictional character from any movie, TV show, comic book, or novel. This modernized version of masking has become increasingly popular over the years and may find a place in your New Year's traditions, although the practice may be reaching cultural oversaturation with its presence at Halloween and various regional pop-culture conventions. Mid-size to large community gatherings can also be the opportunity for local musicians to put on a concert, groups to have fun performing karaoke, or for various kinds of dancing, such as traditional folk, ballroom and swing, or the freeform dances associated with electronic dance music. Any kind of fancy dress party can be as elaborate as your imagination allows, while also

21. Ackerman and Ackerman, *To God Be the Glory*, 152–53.

incorporating the various ways to countdown or commemorate the changing over of the New Year.

One final note: we might say that an unofficial, though widespread, New Year's tradition is to drink our sorrows away through excessive drunkenness and other forms of sensual indulgence. It is worth considering how we might steer others away from this unhealthy form of coping with life's woes, and instead encourage each other, whether in drinking or sobriety, to learn how to feel our hurts and joys together rather than to deludedly medicate them away for a single night.

Making the New Year Sacred

Churches should consider capitalizing on the convergence of the Feast of the Holy Name with New Year's Eve by organizing joint events. Any game night or gala can be preceded earlier on in the evening with a service of prayer, worship, and thanksgiving for God's grace and provision for the year that is past and the year that is to come. One tradition to draw from is the Methodist Watch Night and covenant renewal services that are prominent in African-American congregations and feature calls to recommit ourselves to God in the coming year through extended prayers, singing, and readings which often last through the night until sunrise. The new year is also a time for pastors to begin doing home and family blessings, which is discussed in more detail in the Epiphany chapter, but a New Year's prayer service can feature a special blessing and laying on of hands for the coming year. Your Scripture readings can highlight any passage that emphasize the name of Jesus, such as those mentioned above, but also Philippians 2:5–11, John 14:13, Romans 10:13, 1 Corinthians 6:11, and Isaiah 9:6. With children it is most important to immerse them in exactly what the Holy Family was doing on the eighth day of Christ's birth, and when you feel they are ready, to explain to them what circumcision is. As a reminder, New Year's Eve might be the culmination of your Christmas Vacation Bible School (which are typically in the mornings), or you may want to offer an event night at church that includes its own countdown, but held a few hours earlier than midnight so the kids can get home to bed. Some church communities, who typically do not practice Lenten devotion, take the weeks after the New Year as an opportunity for prayer and fasting for the coming year. Even if your community enters into Lent, you may still want to consider setting aside some time after your New Year's feasting to challenge your community to a season of fasting, praying, and seeking God's face.

As addressed in previous chapters, the challenge of a holiday like New Year's for churches is not so much that they create events which strive for cultural relevancy or that attempt to draw people away from empty worldliness. Instead, their goals should be to discern how to fashion events and rituals filled with both meaning *and* fun, converging the sacred and the secular in such a way that it inspires people to want to celebrate and worship with them year after year. What if our New Year's Eve traditions were filled with the complementary rituals of gathering together to worship, celebratory partying, and, as the new year is dawning, partying that once again erupts into thankful worship for all that God has done? Perhaps it would do us good for our worship to become more celebratory and our celebrations to become more solemn and sacred.

Isn't There a Better Way to do New Year's Resolutions?

The practice of making New Year's resolutions, that is, a list of goals and changes to make in one's life for the coming year, is as much derided as it is valued as a means of changing our behavior. People love to share a slew of self-deprecating jokes, comics, and memes poking fun at how quickly they broke all of their resolutions or how great it is to look back on the past year and realize just how little they actually changed or bettered themselves. As with many traditions surrounding the season, our cynicism leaves us either wanting to abandon the practice of resolutions altogether or to give it a serious rethink. For those of us looking to rethink our resolution practices, here are three suggestions: first, make it a way to honor the elders in our communities, next, make the practice proactively interdependent, and finally, make the practice a sacred covenant where you seek God in prayer as a community about your resolutions.[22]

To the first point, around the world numerous cultures (such as the Netherlands, China, and Quebec) emphasize paying respect to one's elders at the New Year through acts of service and giving them gifts. So, not only may you want to encourage children (of all ages) to find special ways to serve and give gifts to their parents as well as any respected elders in your community, but children can learn to hold themselves accountable by

22. The ideas in this section were adapted and expanded upon from Chaney, *The Twelve Days of Christmas*, "New Year's Day."

presenting their resolutions to their authority figures, either formally or informally. However, our elders can demonstrate their own interdependence and mutual accountability by sharing *their* resolutions for the year with the younger generation. Therefore, a related goal for resolutions would be for everyone to choose attainable goals for which they can be held accountable by your family or group. Along these lines, it is helpful to choose a mutual goal that everyone can agree to do together, such as to exercise at least once a week or to read one book a month. Finally, one way to more firmly resolve to accomplish our resolutions is speak them aloud to each other, pray for and bless each other, and then seek God together who alone gives us the grace to succeed at meeting the humble and fleeting goals we have chosen as a challenge for ourselves. This prayer time could be as simple as coming together as a family, or it could take place at your church's New Year's prayer gathering (as mentioned in the previous section), where perhaps you divide into small groups and share your resolutions with each other and then pray for each other individually before coming back for a more corporate time of worship. Any tradition worthy of keeping is also worthy of serious reform, and a practice like making resolutions, which has so much potential for good but is necessarily derided for its ineffectiveness, is one of the more conventional traditions of the holiday season in dire need of a fresh approach.

Conclusion

New Year's is typically associated as a time for leisure and letting loose, but, as we have done throughout the 12 days, we should be willing to take a risk and steer the cultural narrative toward a mixture of the serious and sacred with the more fun and celebratory. People always look forward to a party, but what if we could create an environment where we equally looked forward to a time on New Year's to reflect, give thanks, come up with goals, and then pray for each other as the former year is coming to a close?

9

Day 12: Feast of the Epiphany and Twelfth Night
(January 5 & 6)

HISTORY AND MEANING

WITH THE FEAST OF the Epiphany on January 6 (or Twelfth Night on January 5) we have another real chance to demonstrate to the broader cultures in which we live just how differently Christmas can come to be celebrated. Even if many of us end up going back to work in the days after Christmas on through the first week of January, and even if the rest of our 12 days contains mostly low-key celebrations at home, we can at least create two festive tent posts worth engaging in with Christmas and

Epiphany. The hope is that people might begin to grasp the vision of what a longer, connected, ongoing 12-day festival might look like.

The story and meaning behind Epiphany was discussed at length in chapter 2, but the key principals to emphasize are that the wise men (or magi) have travelled a great distance and endured great risk to visit Jesus, bestow him with gifts, and worship him. It is also important to center on how through this visitation Jesus is now proclaimed as the King and Savior of the world. The star of Bethlehem lit the way of the wise men, but Jesus is the world's *true* Light, and in him there is no darkness at all (1 John 1:5). In Epiphany the message of the story we began telling in Advent is completed. As the children of Israel we have suffered and endured both physical and spiritual exile from God and neighbor. With Mary, we have longed for and prepared for the Anointed One, the Messiah, our Savior. We have journeyed to Bethlehem and in relative secret beheld his humble arrival with the Holy Family, the angels, shepherds, and whatever animals gathered around. Then, we entered into the trauma of the massacre of the Holy Innocents and the wonder and practicality of his naming and circumcision. Now, at the Epiphany, the whole world metaphorically gathers around Jesus in the form of the wise men and declares "Yes, this is the One we have been waiting for." Our ways of celebrating this feast should allow people the opportunity to fully enter into the joy, long-suffering, and wonder of the narrative we began back at the beginning of December.

For Eastern Orthodox Christians, who commemorate the coming of the magi on December 25 along with the nativity, January 6 is celebrated as the Baptism of Jesus. Often called the Theophany, it is commemorated with the Blessing of the Waters, where a priest, with the town or congregation, will go and bless, pray over, and perhaps throw a wooden cross into a local body of water. In many places water is directly associated with how the people there make their livelihoods and more generally as a source of life.[1] Indeed, on January 5 and 6 water takes a place of prominence in the Orthodox churches, with their liturgies containing a number of Old Testament readings having to do with water—for example, the crossing of the Red Sea, Moses throwing the stick into the water to make it pure, and the account of Moses getting water from the rock. There is also a liturgy to bless holy water for use within the church. This water has various sacramental

1. Miles, *Christmas Customs and Traditions*, 102–3, 344.

uses throughout the year, but the priest also uses it to go do house blessings for the families in his parish up until the beginning of Lent.[2]

With the gift-bringing wise men as their inspiration, in many cultures Epiphany became the primary present-giving day, and you will need to discern (as discussed in chapter 4) if you should either shift giving presents from December 25th to January 6th, divide the present giving equally between the two main feast days of the season, or divide your presents equally among the days. Another option is to of course not emphasize gifts on Epiphany at all and instead focus on the more festive aspects of the feast. As at other times during the 12 days, Epiphany has a number of carnival-like customs associated with it, most likely stemming from the rituals of the Roman Kalends and Saturnalia festivals. Therefore, another area of discernment will be to what extent you want to engage in letting loose at the culmination of the season. However, as with all the recommendations made in this book, our ever-present challenge is to blaze a trail forward that seeks to balance the sacred and secular in a way that is at once holy *and* fun. I will therefore make an argument for an Epiphany that is filled with fun parties and festivals, passionate worship, ornate pageants, and solemnly sweet house blessings.

STRANGE TRADITIONS

A Female Visitor at Epiphany

One tradition worth briefly mentioning is La Befana, the primary gift bringer in Italy, a female figure who takes on similar variations in other countries as the Baboushka (Russia) and Frau Berchta (Germany). Her visit is on the Epiphany every year and her name is an adaptation of that feast name. Her peculiarly fascinating origin myth is that at the time of Christ's birth she was asked by the magi to travel with them to go see the new born king, but she instead "delayed because she wanted to put her house in order before the journey," and as a result she missed seeing Christ altogether.[3] In an act of penance she has since wandered the earth in search of the Christ child and on Epiphany she comes bearing gifts for children as a reminder of her missed opportunity. However, she is also known for leaving bags of ashes, coals, or coming equipped with a stick ready to strike naughty

2. Kishler, unpublished forthcoming interview.
3. Bowler, *Encyclopedia of Christmas*, 19.

children. In this way she mirrors the other Christmas visitors, in that she can at times be benevolent and at other times ready to hand out judgment. What makes La Befana intriguing as a character is her own backstory, which is filled with regret and lament for not being ready to go and meet Jesus when he was born.

The World Turned Upside Down . . . at Christmas

As mentioned in previous chapters, the practice of social inversion, where the weak become strong and people were allowed to switch and play roles opposite from themselves, was prevalent for much of Christmas history. This is another way in which Christmas more closely resembled the customs of Carnival. Through the concealing and transforming power of a mask, costume, painted face, or crossdressing as the opposite gender, someone could temporarily become someone they were not. Taking on different names, such as the Feast of Fools, Feast of the Ass, the Boy Bishop, the Lord of Misrule, and the Abbot of Unreason, those in power were given license to act out in morally risqué ways, and those without power were sometimes given the opportunity to pretend they had command of others. Even so, those truly in charge continued to mock the lower classes in the background.[4] Though these practices either eventually fell out of fashion (at least during Christmas) or were banned altogether due to their unruly and licentious nature, there is something decidedly Christian embedded in their underlying intention to make the last become first, the first become last, where the meek inherit the earth, and the poor in spirit are the inheritors of the kingdom of heaven (Matt 20:16, 5:2–12). The underlying problems with social inversion traditions were that the powerful did not provide any lasting help to the poor and also that these times seemed to be when people felt free to indulge in sinful practices and to take part in bitter and often violent rebellions.

All of this leads us to ask: In what ways might our Christmas practices proclaim the upheaval of Christ's coming to earth, where the most powerful lay aside their authority and make themselves vulnerable, and the weak are lifted up and given place of honor, without devolving into social chaos and immorality? What is more, in what ways can our Christmas traditions go beyond the mere symbol of a temporary social inversion and instead bring

---

4. Bowler, *Encyclopedia of Christmas*, 1, 11–12, 28, 85, 134–35; and Miles, *Christmas Customs and Traditions*, 298, 302–8.

lasting change to our daily lives? We do well to speak of the new order that Christ brings in his coming to earth, but we do even better to show the world how we live out that order, throughout Christmas and every other day of the year. This model of living is what I attempted to lay out in chapter 5, in the section about serving the needs of others during Christmas.

A less high-minded approach to the "foolish" characteristics of these traditions is for us to acknowledge our natural tendencies as a people toward silliness, partying, mischief, practical jokes, dressing up, and pretending we are other people and creatures. We seem to have an innate desire, particularly noticeable around New Year's, to want to let our hair down and let loose through celebrating, and indeed there always seems to be the inevitable reaction to party even more when we are specifically prohibited from doing so. To the extent that it does not betray the life Christ is calling us to live, how might we embrace our propensity for mirth and merrymaking? And how might we come to be known for the annual parties we hold in our homes, community centers, and even churches? My hope is that we can embrace this side of ourselves without devolving into hedonism and chaos, but instead celebrate and even revel in the goodness of God's created order because of the redemption he is bringing about through Jesus.

Time to Wake Up the Apple Trees

While "wassail" often means to drink a toast to someone's good health, and "wassailing" involves going from door to door in your neighborhood with cider or mulled ale—and thus looks a lot like mumming or caroling[5]—wassailing can also mean the superstitious practice of waking up apple trees, who were presumed asleep in the dead of winter, in the hopes of encouraging them to a productive crop in the coming spring and summer. Often occurring on Twelfth Night, a farmer and his family would go into their orchard, fire a gun through the branches of the trees, and sometimes recite a poem, sing a song, or even dance in hopes of awakening the trees to a season of abundant fruitfulness.[6] Over the centuries, many similar customs and their accompanying beliefs arose in hopes of either ensuring the coming harvest season would be plentiful through a set of designated rituals or to divine like a seer how the harvest would turn out. Examples of the latter include the belief that it was good luck for the crops if it snowed on

5. Bowler, *Encyclopedia of Christmas*, 142.
6. Baker, *Discovering Christmas Customs*, 13–14.

Christmas, whereas others believed that the weather during the 12 days acted as a forecast for how the weather would be the remainder of the year.[7] Whatever the customs and the beliefs surrounding them, it is evident they arose from the very real fear that perhaps this year the earth would remain in its dead stillness and not spring to life again once winter departs, and thus they should do everything within their power and discernment to ensure their family would have the food and livelihood necessary to sustain them.

IDEAS FOR CELEBRATING

A Grand Epiphany Festival

In this chapter, the main section of "ideas for celebrating" will be arranged a bit differently than in other chapters. I am going to lay out a single vision for what Twelfth Night and Epiphany can look like for your community, and then afterward include possible variations to consider for the feast. The initial problem when approaching Epiphany is there is possibly too much to fit into a single event, which can include a game night or carnival, the feasting of the King's Cake, the crowning of the Epiphany Kings and Queens, giving out some Epiphany presents, a nativity pageant play, a time of celebratory worship and Communion, and a Christmas tree bonfire. Therefore, it is worth considering *when* exactly you will have your Epiphany celebration. As I see it, there are six options:

- A single combined event on Twelfth Night, January 5, as a feast is technically said to begin in the evening before the feast day.

- A single combined event on the evening of Epiphany, January 6.

- A single combined event on the morning of January 6, though this would most likely alienate anyone who works typical workdays.

- A two-day event that begins on the evening of January 5 with festive celebrating and continues in the morning of January 6 with worship. In this scenario it would make sense for churches to partner with schools and for the celebrations and worship to be located at a school (perhaps right as they are coming back from Christmas break) so children can participate as much as possible. If the fun activities happened

---

7. Baker, *Discovering Christmas Customs*, 24.

the night before and then a relatively brief time of worship, Scripture, and prayer took place first thing in the morning, many parents would still be able to participate as they drop their kids off for school.

- A two-day event where the feast is celebrated on the closest Sunday to the 6th, anywhere from January 2–8, that begins on Saturday evening with festive celebrating and continues the following morning with worship at church.

- A one-day event on the Sunday closest to the 6th, again anywhere from January 2–8, that begins with regular Sunday worship and is followed by festive celebrating during lunchtime. A possible alternative to this would be to break after church and have a Sunday evening festival.

My attempt will be to come up with an event that takes place on a single evening, and thus fits options one or two but could also be adapted for option six (a morning and afternoon). A single event always risks trying to fit too much into a short span of time, but with Epiphany I believe our greater challenge is to create an event that people will find compelling and important enough to fit into their already packed holiday schedules. If Epiphany as a festival becomes more popular over the years, people may begin to *desire* to make it a two-day event, but if we are going to risk attempting to convince people to make their Christmas season longer (by essentially creating an entirely new holiday for them), we should be willing to make it as accessible as possible for them. However, if you decide to always hold your event on that first Saturday evening and Sunday morning of January (after the New Year) people may be more open to having an expanded version of the feast, as weekend events are more easy to fit into our schedules.

The kind of event I am suggesting would last about three and a half hours, though it could be expanded to last longer. It most naturally fits into a church community setting, mixing fun activities with joyous worship, though it could be adapted for a school or scaled down for a house group or family. Here's a simple timeline for the evening:[8]

---

8. Though most of these traditions are are universal enough to Twelfth Night and Epiphany or the winter holidays in general, the ideas in this section, unless specifically noted, were culled from Ackerman and Ackerman, *To God Be the Glory*, 154–56; Chaney, *The Twelve Days of Christmas*, sections "The Meaning of Epiphany," "Epiphany in the Parish," and "Epiphany in the Home"; and Miles, *Christmas Customs and Traditions*, 337–50.

- 5:30 p.m.–6:30: an hour for group games, carnival games, and contests

- 6:30 p.m.–7:15: a time to pass out the King's Cake, discover the winners, pass out gifts, and fifteen minutes of buffer time to prepare for worship

- 7:30 p.m.—8:45: a time for a nativity pageant performance and worship

- 9:00 p.m.: a Christmas Tree Bonfire

Broken down into more detail, the first hour of your evening will feature a time for games and competitions. As with other game times, you have nearly endless options at your disposal. A smaller or more low-key church may want to have card and board games available, but you could arrange various group games, sports, silly contests, auctions, or raffle drawings. Another option is to rent or build your own set of carnival games and make the evening feel like a fair. The retro route is also a possibility, where you institute the tradition of playing a set of truly classic Christmas and Twelfth Night games. Some of these games include Blind Man's Bluff, Feed the Dove, Hot-cockles, Yawning for a Cheshire Cheese, Snap Dragon,[9] and the forfeit games that were described in chapter 1 and notably associated with the 12 days of Christmas song. Descriptions of many other older games can be found in a volume like *Jolly Games for Happy Homes*.[10] Of course you will need to look up the rules of these games in order to learn how to play them faithfully or to at least adapt them to a modern setting. This hour can be either organized around group games that everyone is encouraged to participate in, organized around a single sporting event or competition that some participate in and others observe as an audience, or organized as a kind of open house where the games are operated by volunteers and people are allowed to float freely and choose how much time they spend at each station.

At around the hour mark you will transition to the first major combined event of the evening, the eating of the King's Cake and the selection of the Epiphany King(s) and Queen(s). In making the King's Cake, of which there are a number of culinary variations to choose from as well as ways to decorate, the idea is to first hide in the pre-baked batter either a bean, a plastic baby figurine, a coin (real or plastic), or plastic representations of the three gifts of the wise men. Then, when the time comes, slice up the

9. Bowler, *Encyclopedia of Christmas,* 88.
10. Clark, *Jolly Games for Happy Homes.*

cake and hand out the slices at random, and whoever finds the bean(s) or other objects becomes the Epiphany Kings or Queens. Going in to your dessert lottery you will need to determine first which object(s) you want to use and how many, depending on the number of Kings or Queens you will make winners. Second, you should determine if you want just one winner, one boy and one girl winner, three total winners, or another variation of your choosing. Then you will need to decide if this is a game only for children or if adults will play as well, and if the chances to win are equal for all age groups. Finally, you need to consider what the evening's privileges are for the Kings and Queens. Historically, the winners became the Kings and Queens of Epiphany, the King of Misrule, or the Boy Bishop, and would act as a kind of master of ceremonies for the evening or for the duration of the festival. They would be given certain temporary rights and even be allowed to command others. For our sake, my recommendations for privileges are that they be presented with a crown and possibly a costume through a mock coronation ceremony and then be given a prize. You could also give them the authority to pass gifts out to everyone else, as well as the possibility of acting in the evening's upcoming nativity play as the wise men. As gifts for the Kings and Queens to pass out, you might have chocolate candy coins, prepackaged desserts, or a small toy. If you reward your newly christened monarchs with the privilege of being the wise men in the nativity play, they will require some stage instructions or at the very least will need to be able to understand how to follow along with the more rehearsed actors. On the other hand, you may choose to reserve parts for the wise men only to the actors who have taken the time to rehearse and prepare. Finally, though you can certainly give your Kings and Queens grand authority and decision-making powers over your Epiphany festivities, it may be best to steer away from those kinds of traditions, unless you are willing to endure the consequences of monarchs who eventually make exorbitant, unfair, or socially awkward and embarrassing demands.

Assuming you can take care of the King's Cake, the crowning, and the gift giving in about a half an hour, the next event of your night would be to have a time of worship and to put on a nativity play. As suggested in chapter 7, you might consider having children begin rehearsing a Christmas pageant on Holy Innocents' Day and continue throughout your Christmas VBS on up to the day of the performance. A play can range from ambitious and astute depending on your staging and script, to sweetly simple depending on how young your actors are. Scripts can be purchased—though there are some worthy public domain Christmas plays—or you can write one yourself. Your time of worship will also vary depending on your tradition and however you envision your Epiphany liturgy. My encouragement would be to focus on where we are in the narrative of Christ's birth, to emphasize Christ as Savior of the world (for all people) and that the nations came to *him*. I also recommend holding off on singing some of the more Epiphany-themed carols (or at least specific verses of those carols until January 5 or 6), which would include "We Three Kings," "What Child is This?" and "The First Noel."

After worship your evening could have a grand conclusion in the form of a bonfire, especially one that features burning everyone's (natural) Christmas trees. Although in some traditions families leave their decorations up until Candlemas on February 2, a large amount of people already begin taking down decorations by January 1. A tree-burning would therefore help to aid families with a visceral reminder that the 12 days have come to an end and that we can together create a bright (and hot) visual reminder that Christ is the Light of the world. It is worth mentioning however that bonfires should be done in approved areas and may need to be moved away from the church and to someone's home in the country, otherwise you risk having local police or fire departments pay you an unwanted visit. If your church has adequate space for a bonfire, you could preempt any difficulties by intentionally inviting police and firefighters or at least making them aware of what you are doing with a simple phone call. Not everyone buys natural Christmas trees for their decorations, so you could welcome people to bring any firewood and boxes to contribute to the blaze. A fire (especially a large one) is another event that people will begin to look forward to with anticipation year after year, and it is also one rooted in (or adapted from) a number of older Christmas, New Year's, and Epiphany traditions.

Miscellaneous Suggestions

The idea with Twelfth Night and Epiphany is to create an event that draws people in through a carefully crafted mixture of celebration and worship, contests, pageantry, and good old fashioned pyrotechnics. There are other adaptations to consider, so here are a few miscellaneous suggestions:

- For the sake of the tone and posture of your event you may very well want to split up your Epiphany festival from your Epiphany worship into two events held at separate times. There is certainly wisdom in such an approach, though you may find it difficult to gather people at both events. For some communities it might make the most sense to plan your festival, nativity play, and bonfire for a Saturday evening and then allow Sunday morning (January 2–8) to specifically focus on worship and teaching about Epiphany.

- When decorating both your party and worship spaces consider having lots of silver and gold stars hanging in places, some of which the children could make as a project at the CVBS, Holy Family Sunday, or your New Year's party. You could also set up a great many safely positioned candles and decorative lights that differ from your Christmas lighting. Other decorations to consider are depictions and statues of the wise men and their three gifts. As a historical and visceral lesson you could have someone with actual gold, frankincense, and myrrh for people to touch and smell.

- Whether for your church or family, now is the time to update your nativity set with the wise men. As you did with the Holy Family, it is fun to move them closer as January 6 approaches. You could even make placing the wise men in the nativity how your Epiphany festival gets started, and it can be the privileged duty of the King and Queen of Epiphany. Another possible addition to your nativity is to transform it into a throne for the king, "enthroning" it with a crown on Christ, accenting it with royally colored fabrics, placing a golden scepter in Christ's hand, and possibly replacing his manger with a throne. I do believe though it is important to consider how our portrayals of Christ mix his divinity and authority with his humility and humanity. As one who came to serve, perhaps we should crown Christ on Epiphany while still leaving him in his unadorned manger.

- Many cultures enjoy a piñata for Epiphany (or New Year's), but pretty much every culture enjoys hitting a cardboard decoration filled with candy and prizes! If you have a lot of children you could even have three piñatas held by each of the three wise men or by the Epiphany Kings and Queens. This tradition could become a centerpiece to your Epiphany festival.

- You may want to consider having your wise men pre-chosen either from middle-aged and older members of the church or from the actors playing them in the pageant play, and then have them come out as gift bringers similar to Santa Claus. This would make them a more mysterious addition to your Epiphany festival, and it would also differentiate them from the Epiphany King and Queen elected through the cake contest. In some countries, such as in Spain and Italy, the wise men were the *actual* Christmas or Epiphany visitors that children magically believed delivered their presents, so you are always welcome to attempt to bring back this practice as a tradition![11]

- One way to represent the coming together of the nations is to include a meal with dishes from around the world. While this may not fit a carnival aesthetic, your Epiphany evening could feature a meal where everyone in your church brings an entrée or dessert from their own cultural heritage or a food from a culture they love.

- Though separate from the main Epiphany events, a good recommendation for church staffs and house groups is to hold off on having their official "Christmas" parties until after the New Year or even after Epiphany. With all the busyness of the season, it is helpful to allow a few days to pass and then have a relaxed party amongst leaders anytime throughout Christmastide, especially once people's schedules have slowed down.

- An additional idea that works well during a church-staff or small-group Twelfth Night party is for everyone to bring something special to share, such as a poem, a reading, a picture, a story from their life, a song, or any artifact of meaning to them. At some point everyone takes their turn and shares what they have brought while the party's hosts relate how our gifts are like those of the wise men, who humbly brought their offerings in honor of the King.

- As a way of getting in an extra rehearsal for the nativity play, your group could arrange for a performance sometime before the 6th at a children's hospital, nursing home, group home, school, or any group you think would be blessed with watching a Christmas play.

- There are also caroling/mumming/wassailing traditions associated with Epiphany, which you would be welcome to institute, such as the Star Boys practice—different from the St. Lucia Day tradition—of young people who dress up as the wise men and follow around a star on a pole as they parade from house to house and, per usual, sing

---

11. Miles, *Christmas Customs and Traditions*, 343.

carols, mischievously knock on doors as a prank, and then ask each house for money or refreshments.[12]

- As in previous chapters, most, if not all, of these ideas are scalable for a Twelfth Night and Epiphany party in your home. Even though many of the 12 days have already been suggested as game nights, you could have another gaming party in your home with traditional Twelfth Night games or any game of your choosing. Relatedly, your children (along with other families) can help put on a nativity play, you can do your own King's Cake and crowning of the King and Queen, you can worship, sing carols and read Scripture, and you can have your own bonfire all on your own property.

Epiphany House Blessings

As a possible adaptation of the Blessing of the Waters and the house blessings in the Eastern Orthodox churches, a number of Western traditions have instituted their own Epiphany house blessings. Since Epiphany is not the feast of Christ's baptism in the Western churches it may not make much sense to have a blessing of the waters, though it would be a way for the West to work toward liturgical, seasonal, and sacramental solidarity with the East. However, it would also make sense for the church to agree upon a single day for Christ's baptism (this Western Christian author thinks the Sunday following Epiphany makes the most sense) and so practice water and home blessings together at the same time. For those of us in the West our options are to either practice a more Epiphany-focused house blessing around the 6th of January or a more water- and baptismal-focused house blessing starting a week later around Christ's baptism on the 13th of January. Both practices are typically done in the window between Epiphany and Candlemas on February 2, though I do not see why the blessings could not be started any time around the new year as a way of accommodating people's schedules.

While it makes the most sense for a priest, pastor, or someone in church leadership to do the house blessing, the parents of a household or an individual could do their own, though, as with any recommendation in this book, traditions are best practiced within community. In a sense, during the house blessing, the leader takes on the role of the wise men,

12. Bowler, *Encyclopedia of Christmas*, 214.

who pilgrimaged to Christ and offered blessings in the form of gifts and worship. As a way of signifying the year, a family takes chalk and above the main entryway to their home (or as many doors as they choose) they write the first two numbers of the new year, followed by the initials of both the traditional names of the wise men (being Caspar, Melchior, and Balthasar) and the Latin phrase *Christus mansionem benedicat* (which means "Christ bless this house"), followed by the last two numbers of the new year. Plus signs are included in between each letter and digit. An example for the year 2081 would be: 20+C+M+B+81. The church leader would then pray a pre-written or spontaneous blessing over the family and their home, blessing it with water or anointing oils.

One variation on this tradition is to have a group (typically three) dressed up as the magi and for *them* to go around to a community's houses and write the chalk inscriptions. Oftentimes, as in the other processing rituals, the hosts would bless the visitors with refreshments or money, whereas in other instances the "kings" would come with gifts to pass out to everyone.[13]

Stations of the Nativity

One idea all churches should consider implementing is to commission a "Stations of the Nativity" (or Epiphany) as a parallel to the Stations of the Cross.[14] Many churches already offer guided prayers and Scripture readings of the Stations of the Cross during Holy Week, but one option would be to take those down from Advent through Epiphany (or until Candlemas) and then offer a time during the 12 days or on Epiphany to guide a group through the stations with a set of prayers, Scripture readings, and reflections to match the nativity art. Alternatively the works could be placed in another section of the nave, a side chapel, or another place in the church altogether. The idea, similar to the Jesse tree or Lessons and Carols, is to give people a chance to hear the full narrative of Christ's coming while also seeing it depicted through the visual power of art. Liturgically, this would create another artistic and symbolic center of prominence in your place of worship, a commemoration of the incarnation to mirror that of the Passion.

13. Though Epiphany house blessings are a common practice, more details and suggestions can be found at Skojec, "The Chalking of the Doors"; and Chaney, *The Twelve Days of Christmas*, "Blessing of the Home."

14. Gunstone, *Christmas and Epiphany*, 96.

This would also be a prime opportunity to support local artists in your area by commissioning them to paint, draw, or sculpt the stations. Two devotional books are available, both entitled *Stations of the Nativity*, that feature slightly varied options for the fourteen stations and can be utilized and adapted for both the home and church setting.[15]

15. Chapman, *Stations of the Nativity*; and Boadt, *Stations of the Nativity*.

CONCLUSION

Mapping Out Your Christmas

Now that we have toured through the various traditions and feast days at our disposal it is time for you to map out what you want your 12 days to look like. Whether you are leading your family, your church community, or another social group, I invite you to take some time to dream and plan and begin communicating to people what a longer Christmas season could look like in your context. Be aware that significant cultural shifts are often incremental and thus you will need to consider *how* you want to communicate about all the grand changes you want to start implementing. It might prove to be the most fruitful to begin having conversations with your church leadership and family members sometime in the months leading up to Christmas, perhaps even in the summer time. This way you will give people ample opportunity to acclimate themselves to your ideas and to make plans together as a united community rather than to be seen as a lone wolf attempting to make extreme changes to everyone's "normal" Christmas. Attempt to communicate in a non-threatening manner, perhaps using a system like Nonviolent Communication,[1] where you make your observation about the current way you celebrate Christmas as a community, you state how that makes you feel, you next list your needs for how you *want* Christmas to be celebrated, and then you make your requests for change. Reforming people's long held traditions is difficult for any group, but if you can make your proposal in an inviting way, it might be possible to implement a 12 days of Christmas plan in one big step: "Hey everyone, what if we tried to do a full 12 days of Christmas festival? I've thought about it and have come up with a plan for us to consider."

After contemplating your approach, your next step is to think about the scope of the 12 days itself. The options are laid out in the previous chapters, but you will need to make the following decisions. First, choose to what extent you will engage in the individual saints' days and how much you will relate them to Christmas. Then discern whether your community will gather for worship and prayer on all of the days, only key selected days, or only on the tent posts of Christmas Day and Epiphany, while encouraging personal or family devotions for the rest of days. Next, you should decide whether you will focus mostly on Christmas Day and Epiphany when it comes to larger events or if you will plan numerous gathered social events throughout the season. It is also worth considering what old or new practices that are foreign in your context you will attempt to institute and begin encouraging your people to try. Finally, as emphasized throughout this book you need to discern to what extent your season will balance and intertwine worship, celebration, service, and leisure.

Map it out, make your proposals, be willing to compromise as your community begins to wrap its head around a new understanding of Christmas, and continually be a joyful, encouraging advocate for celebrating Christ's birth as a glorious 12-day season. Follow your instincts as you consider how to adapt past rituals for your modern context, and remember, you are essentially remaking Christmas, even as you attempt to rediscover how it was celebrated in the past.

---

1. Rosenberg, *Nonviolent Communication*.

AFTERWORD

Embracing the Paradoxes of Christmas

THERE ARE MANY PARADOXES, some would say contradictions, worth contemplating surrounding Christ's birth and the holiday of Christmas. A paradox, as I have come to know it, is when two contradictory truths converge and somehow create an even deeper truth. Christmas, then, is profoundly and innately paradoxical. Though the logical tensions of the holiday are difficult for many to accept, creating much cognitive and moral dissonance, perhaps it is the joyful convergence of its many contradictions that cause us to so fondly long for this time of the year.

To start with, in Christmas we seem stuck between the polar tensions to either make the holiday "what you want" or to follow the grand traditions of the past. There is a somewhat prevalent modern sentiment that in order for Christmas to be special we have to discover the practices that work best for "you": *your* life, *your* family, *your* world—of which *you* are the very center (which is a paradox in and of itself). From this perspective, the greatest Christmas is the one that fits you best, as if traditions and celebrations are only as relevant as they are tailor-made to suit individuals or individual families. The opposite of this sentiment is to rely heavily on the long-held traditions handed down throughout the generations. On the less personal side of the paradox, we do not follow the preferences of our own hearts but rather adhere to the practices of an established authority, in this case the church or a shared national, ethnic, or familial heritage. It is too easy to give in to the either/or temptations of individualism or traditionalism when the truth is that we will have our best Christmases when these sentiments converge. We should openly acknowledge that our Christmas celebrations will continually be adapted, added to, and forgotten, and thus we are *always* in the process of making the holiday "work" for our particular context. Culture is not static, and we put undue pressure on ourselves by attempting to adhere to a strict unchanging tradition. And yet, there is an emptiness in the present culture's idolization of the new and novel. When we follow a tradition that extends back throughout the generations our worship and celebrating transcends time itself, where our Christmas in the present is a beautiful, meaningful resounding echo of Christmases past. Here, the truth of the paradox is that our modern-day Christmas become the most meaningful when we take the traditions of the past and give them new life, new meaning, and even new adaptations in the present. A Christmas that is most alive will always be both *of* the past and *in* the present. Christmas truly is "what we make it," but it is still up to us to ensure that the traditions of the past continue to live on in future generations.

One of the most conflicting Christmas contradictions is the tension in the question, "Is Christmas a sacred or a secular holiday?" For Christians the answer is most definitely that it is "sacred," and still we continually lament how much this time of year has been co-opted by the secular and commercialistic components of the holiday. And yet, only the most puritanical among us would deny that we truly enjoy and even are enriched by the "secular" parts of Christmas. While it is certainly a legitimate concern that silly, sentimental Christmas movies, sporting events, playing board games, and the onslaught of new toys can draw us away from the worship of the Savior, they can also draw us closer together if we are intentional about how we enter into them. The truth found in the sacred/secular paradox, and this is where secularism inevitably loses out (or is transformed entirely), is that God can sanctify and be honored in our fun and leisure, and thus even the "secular" can become holy in its own way, where "Secularism isn't an abandonment of the sacred. The secular is finding that the ordinary *is* sacred."[1] As opposed to a rigid legalism that would seek to make the 12-day season one long succession of solemn worship and prayer services, this paradoxical understanding of Christmas sees our game playing, our myth telling, and yes even our secular Christmas song singing as acts of worship before God, so long as we deliberately live our lives holding to the tension that God can be glorified in all things. Christians always seem to get trapped into protesting the vices of Christmas, but perhaps we would do better to instead begin joyfully injecting and transforming some of its secular traditions with elements of the sacred, even as we continue to invite people into our times of worship.

The greatest paradoxes of Christmas involve Christ himself. These are the true wonders surrounding his coming, the mysteries that are thankfully beyond our comprehension and thus continually invite our pondering. First and foremost we must always keep before us the glorious and (for some) offensive nature of Christ's incarnation, how God became flesh and dwelt among us (John 1:14). Our minds cannot conceive how the Lord who made heaven and earth can be contained in a single human body, and yet our Christmas worship humbly acknowledges the mysteries of the paradox, as described in the words of the Council of Chalcedon, which I encourage us to approach as much as a poem as a theological treatise. In it Jesus is described as:

> "truly God and truly a human being . . . coessential with the Father as to his deity and coessential with us . . . as to his humanity, being like us in every respect apart from sin. As to his deity, he was born from the Father before the ages, but as to his humanity, the very same one was born in the last days from the Virgin Mary, the Mother of God, for our sake and the sake of our salvation: one and the same Christ, Son, Lord, Only Begotten, acknowledged to be unconfusedly, unalterably, undividedly, inseparably in two natures . . . not divided or torn into two persons but one and the same Son and only-begotten God, Logos, Lord Jesus Christ."[2]

1. Peters, "The Incarnation Changes Everything."
2. Norris, "The Council of Chalcedon's," 159.

Funnily enough, I believe the Church Fathers needed so many and varied words to make up their "definition" of Christ, because it is essentially a mystery too profound for words. Still, we find ourselves compelled to try.

Bound up in the paradox of Christ's incarnation is the tension of whether or not, in the newborn Jesus, we are worshipping a baby. While some traditions have arisen that fixate on worshipping an infant version of Christ, creating statuary and iconography as objects of their devotion, I believe it is key to remember that when Jesus was a baby he was the eternal Logos, the begotten Son of God, and the eventual crucified, risen, and reigning Savior of the world. There is no baby to worship, there is only the God-man, Jesus Christ, who at one time was a baby. And herein lies the last mystery worth noting, as some of our Christmas carols remind us every year: that the way of the cross was present in Christ's birth, that he was born to lay down his life for us: "Nails, spear shall pierce him through, / the cross he bore for me for you. / Hail, hail the Word made flesh, / the Babe the Son of Mary."[3]

Since Christ himself stepped into the tensions of an earthly existence, thus making it holy, we too should seek to hold the contradictions of Christmas in tension, as doing so will lead us not only into profound and solemn worship but also jovial fun, serving the needs of people in our world, and everything in between.

3. William C. Dix, "What Child is This?"

APPENDIX

A List of Christmas Stories, Plays, Sermons, and Reflections

As SUGGESTED A FEW times in this book, the Christmas season (whether you are an introvert or an extrovert) can be a great time to cuddle up with a book in a secluded corner of your house or to read passages aloud to each other through the dark winter nights. Provided here is a non-comprehensive list of various Christmas-themed books. I have attempted to include a variety of sources, some of which were cited in the book and some of which I had hoped to cite but could not find a way to fit them in. The readings are both ancient and modern, some are devotional or heavily theological, while others are silly and secular. I have included short stories, plays, novels, children's books, and sermons, along with some books that are extended reflections on the meaning of the season.

Alcott, Louisa May et al. *A Vintage Christmas: A Collection of Classic Stories and Poems*. Nashville: Thomas Nelson, 2018.

Allsburg, Chris Van. *The Polar Express*. Boston: Houghton Mifflin, 1985.

Andersen, Hans Christian. "The Fir Tree." Berkeley, CA: Ten Speed, 2016.

———. "The Little Match Girl." Multiple publishers.

———. "The Snow Queen." Berkeley, CA: Ten Speed, 2016.

Athanasius, St. *On the Incarnation*. Translated by A Religious of C.S.M.V. Crestwood, NY: St. Vladimir's Seminary, 1993.

Augustine. *Sermons for Christmas and Epiphany*. Translated by Thomas Comerford Lawler. New York: Newman, 1952.

Baum, Frank L. *The Life and Adventures of Santa Claus*. Multiple publishers.

Bernard of Clairvaux. *Sermons for Advent and the Christmas Season*. Leinenweber, John, ed. Translated by Irene Edmonds, Wendy Mary Beckett, and Conrad Greenia. Kalamazoo, MI: Cistercian, 2007.

Boadt, Lawrence. *Stations of the Nativity*. Mahwah, NJ: Paulist, 2016.

Bonhoeffer, Dietrich. *God in the Manger: Reflections on Advent and Christmas*. Louisville, KY: Westminster John Knox, 2012.

Buck, Pearl S. *Christmas Day in the Morning*. New York: Harper Collins, 2002.

Capote, Truman. *A Christmas Memory*. New York: Modern Library, 1996.

Carter, Albert Howard. *For Magi, Shepherds, and Us*. Illustrated by Robert O. Hodgell. Richmond, VA: John Knox, 1970.

Chapman, Raymond. *Stations of the Nativity: Meditations on the Incarnation of Christ*. New York: Morehouse, 1999.

Dickens, Charles. *A Christmas Carol*. Multiple publishers.

———. *Christmas Stories*. The Oxford Illustrated Dickens. Oxford: Oxford University Press, 1987.

Doyle, Arthur Conan et al. *The Valancourt Book of Victorian Christmas Ghost Stories*. Vols. 1–3. Richmond, VA: Valancourt, 2016–2018.

English, Adam C. *Christmas: Theological Anticipations*. Eugene, OR: Cascade, 2016.

Ephrem the Syrian, *Hymns and Homilies of St. Ephraim the Syrian*. Scotts Valley, CA: Createspace, 2012.

Evans, Richard Paul. *The Christmas Box Collection: The Christmas Box, Timepiece, and the Letter*. New York: Simon and Schuster, 1998.

Smith, Dean Lambert. *The Advent Jesse Tree: Devotions for Children and Adults to Prepare for the Coming of the Christ Child at Christmas*. Nashville: Abingdon, 2010.

Freeman, Emily Belle. *Celebrating a Christ-centered Christmas: Seven Traditions to Lead Us Closer to the Savior*. Salt Lake: Ensign Peak, 2010.

Gogol, Nikolai. *The Night Before Christmas*. London: Penguin, 2014.

Guite, Malcolm. *Waiting on the Word: A poem a day for Advent, Christmas and Epiphany*. London: Canterbury, 2015.

Haidle, Helen. *The 12 Days of Christmas*. Illustrated by Laura Knorr. Grand Rapids: Zonderkidz, 2003.

Heinz, Donald. *Christmas: Festival of Incarnation*. Minneapolis: Fortress, 2010.

Henry, O. "The Gift of the Magi." Multiple publishers.

Hoffmann, E. T. A. *The Nutcracker and the Mouse King*. Multiple publishers.

Houselander, Caryll. *The Reed of God*. Notre Dame, IN: Christian Classics, 2006.

Keane, James, eds. et al. *Goodness and Light: Readings for Advent and Christmas*. Maryknoll, NY: Orbis, 2015

Keller, Timothy. *Hidden Christmas: The Surprising Truth behind the Birth of Christ*. New York: Viking, 2016.

Köstenberger, Andreas J. and Alexander Stewart. *The First Days of Jesus: The Story of the Incarnation*. Wheaton, IL: Crossway, 2015.

Lewis, C. S. "A Christmas Sermon for Pagans." *VII* 34 (2017) 46–50.

———. "Xmas and Christmas" and "What Christmas Means to Me." In *God in the Dock*, 301–305. Grand Rapids: Eerdmans, 1970.

Mosteller, Angie. *Christmas: Celebrating the Christian History of Classic Symbols, Songs and Stories*. USA: Holiday Classics, 2010.

Pennover, Greg, and Gregory Wolfe, eds. *God with Us: Rediscovering the Meaning of Christmas*. Brewster, MA: Paraclete 2007.

Pepper, Dennis. *An Oxford Book of Christmas Stories*. Toronto: Oxford University Press, 1986.

Robinson, Barbara. *The Best Christmas Pageant Ever*. New York: Harper Collins, 2005.

Shakespeare, William. *Twelfth Night*. Multiple publishers.

———. *The Winter's Tale*. Multiple publishers.

Spurgeon, Charles H. *Joy Born at Bethlehem: 19 Christmas Sermons from the Ministry of Charles Spurgeon*. Shawnee, KS: Primedia, 2013.

Stiegemeyer, Julia. *Saint Nicholas: The Real Story of the Christmas Legend.* Illustrated by Chris Ellison. Saint Louis: Concordia, 2003.

Toal, M. F., ed. and trans. *Patristic Homilies on the Gospels: From the First Sunday of Advent to Quinquagesima.* Vol. 1. Chicago: Henry Regent Company, 1955.

Tolkien, J. R. R. *Letters from Father Christmas.* Baillie Tolkien, ed. London: Harper Collins, 2015.

Trollope, Anthony. *Christmas at Thompson Hall: And Other Christmas Stories.* London: Penguin, 2014.

Twain, Mark. "A Letter From Santa Claus." Multiple publishers.

Weintraub, Stanley. *Silent Night: The Story of the World War I Christmas Truce.* New York: Plume, 2002.

Wojciechowski, Susan. *The Christmas Miracle of Jonathan Toomey.* Illustrated by P. J. Lynch. Sommerville, MA: Candlewick, 2015

Bibliography

Ackerman, Keith L., and Joann Ackerman. *To God Be the Glory: Growing Towards a Healthy Church (A Workbook for Clergy and Laity)*. Quincy, IL: DoveTracts, 2001.

Adam, Adolf. *The Liturgical Year: Its History and Its Meaning after the Reform of the Liturgy*. Collegeville, MN: Pueblo, 1981.

Alexander, J. Neil. *Waiting for the Coming: The Liturgical Meaning of Advent, Christmas, Epiphany*. Church Year. Washington, DC: Pastoral, 1993.

Anderson, E. Byron. Unpublished forthcoming interview. Interviewed by Chris Marchand. June 2018.

Appleton, Joanne. "Mid Sized Mission: The Use of Mid Size Groups as a Vital Strategic Component of Church Planting." European Church Planting Network, 2008. https://www.christianitytoday.com/assets/10233.pdf

Ard, Natalie. *The Christmas Star from Afar*. Alamo, CA: Star Kids, 2015.

Ashton, John. *A Righte Merrie Christmasse: The Story of Christ-Tide*. London: Leadenhall, 1894.

Ashton, John. *Studying John: Approaches to the Fourth Gospel*. Clarendon, 1994.

Austin, Frederic. "The Twelve Days of Christmas." London: Novello, 1909.

Bailey, Kenneth E. *Jesus through Middle Eastern Eyes*. Downers Grove: InterVarsity, 2008.

Baker, Margaret. *Discovering Christmas Customs and Folklore*. Princes Risborough, UK: Shire, 1999.

Baring-Gould, William S., and Ceil Baring-Gould. *The Annotated Mother Goose*. Seaton, UK: Bramhall House, 1962.

Beckwith, Roger T. "St. Luke, the Date of Christmas and the Priestly Courses at Qumran." *Revue de Qumrân* 9.1 (1977) 73–94.

Beers, V. Gilbert. *The Savior: The Birth and Early Life of Jesus*. The Book of Life 17. Grand Rapids: Zondervan, 1980.

Bernard of Clairvaux. *Sermons for Advent and the Christmas Season*. Edited by John Leinenweber. Translated by Irene Edmonds et al. Kalamazoo, MI: Cistercian, 2007.

Boadt, Lawrence. *Stations of the Nativity*. Mahwah, NJ: Paulist, 2016.

Bowler, Gerry. *The World Encyclopedia of Christmas*. Toronto: McClelland & Stewart, 2000.

Bradshaw, Paul F., and Maxwell E. Johnson. *The Origins of Feasts, Fasts, and Seasons in Early Christianity*. Collegeville, MN: Liturgical, 2011.

Briganti, Paul, dir. *Adam Ruins Everything*. Season 1, episode 1, "Adam Ruins Giving." Tru TV. September, 2015.

Brown, Raymond E. *The Birth of the Messiah: A Commentary on the Infancy Narratives in the Gospels of Matthew and Luke.* The Anchor Yale Bible Reference Library. New Haven: Yale University Press, 1999.

———. *The Gospel According to John I–XII.* Anchor Bible Series 29. Garden City, NY: Doubleday, 1966.

Carlson, Stephen C. "The Accommodations of Joseph and Mary in Bethlehem: κατάλυμα in Luke 2.7." *New Testament Studies* 56 (2010) 326–42.

Chaney, Elsa. *The Twelve Days of Christmas.* Collegeville, MN: Liturgical, 1955. https://www.ewtn.com/catholicism/library/twelve-days-of-christmas-10410.

Chapman, Raymond. *Stations of the Nativity: Meditations on the Incarnation of Christ.* Harrisburg, PA: Morehouse, 1999.

"Christmas: December 27th; Feast of St. John, apostle and evangelist." https://www.catholicculture.org/culture/liturgicalyear/calendar/day.cfm?date=2018–12-27.

Clark, Georgianna C. *Jolly Games for Happy Homes.* London: Dean & Son, 1876.

Collins, Ace. *Stories behind the Best-loved Songs of Christmas.* Grand Rapids: Zondervan, 2001.

Connell, Martin. "Did Ambrose's Sister Become a Virgin on December 25 or January 6? The Earliest Western Evidence for Christmas and Epiphany outside Rome." *Studia Liturgica* 29 (1999) 145–58.

———. *On God and Time, Advent, Christmas, Epiphany, Candlemas.* Eternity Today: On the Liturgical Year 1. New York: Continuum, 2006.

Corbett, Steve, and Brian Fikkert. *When Helping Hurts: How to Alleviate Poverty without Hurting the Poor . . . and Yourself.* Chicago: Moody, 2012.

Davis, Susan G. "'Making Night Hideous': Christmas Revelry and Public Order in Nineteenth-Century Philadelphia." *American Quarterly* 34.2 (1982), 185–199.

de la Mare, Guinevere. "Jolabokaflod: Meet Your Favorite New Holiday Tradition." https://www.readitforward.com/essay/article/jolabokaflod-meet-favorite-new-holiday-tradition/

Deems, Edward M. *Holy Days and Holidays: A Treasury of Historical Material, Sermons in Full and in Brief, Suggestive Thoughts, and Poetry, Relating to Holy Days and Holidays.* New York: Funk & Wagnalls, 1906.

Dickey, Colin. "A Plea to Resurrect the Christmas Tradition of Telling Ghost Stories." https://www.smithsonianmag.com/history/plea-resurrect-christmas-tradition-telling-ghost-stories-180967553/?fbclid=IwAR0ECXYtnf_hZcsXue7JnUCh6h-jiMXAS8fSayCG3UnVLSowDK7XfYkk9fI#5AxLpp6FIHYz9IrF.01.

Dunbar, R. I. M. "Neocortex Size as a Constraint on Group Size in Primates." *Journal of Human Evolution* 22.6 (1992) 469-93.

Farley, David. *An Irreverent Curiosity: In Search of the Church's Strangest Relic in Italy's Oddest Town.* New York: Avery, 2010.

Ferguson, George. *Signs and Symbols in Christian Art.* Oxford: Oxford University Press, 1954.

"A Festival of Nine Lessons and Carols." http://www.kings.cam.ac.uk/events/chapel-services/nine-lessons.html.

Filz, Gretchen, "Does Christmas End on Epiphany?" www.catholiccompany.com/getfed/does-christmas-end-on-epiphany-5962.

———. "The Symbolism of the 3 Christmas Masses." https://www.catholiccompany.com/getfed/symbolism-christmas-masses-6178.

Foote, G. W., and J. M. Wheeler. *Crimes of Christianity.* Berlin, OH: TGS, 2005.

Ghanem, Heba. "Refugee Tales: Walking in Solidarity." https://refugeeweek.org.uk/refugee-tales-walking-in-solidarity/.

Gibson, David J. "The Date of Christ's Birth." *Bible League Quarterly*. October/December 1965. http://nabataea.net/birthdate.html.

Golby, J. M., and A. W. Purdue. *The Making of the Modern Christmas*. Athens, GA: University of Georgia Press, 1986.

Gomme, Alice Bertha. *The Traditional Games of England, Scotland, and Ireland, x. 1*. London: David Nutt, 1894.

Gunstone, John. *Christmas and Epiphany*. London: Faith, 1967.

Hervey, Thomas K. *The Book of Christmas: Descriptive of the Customs, Ceremonies, Traditions, Superstitions, Fun, Feeling, and Festivities of the Christmas Season*. Boston: Roberts Brothers, 1888.

Hijmans, Steven. "Sol Invictus, the Winter Solstice, and the Origins of Christmas." *Mouseion* 3.3 (2003) 377–98.

Holweck, Frederick. "Holy Innocents." In *The Catholic Encyclopedia 7*. New York: Robert Appleton, 1910. http://www.newadvent.org/cathen/07419a.htm.

"Holy Innocents." https://www.franciscanmedia.org/holy-innocents/.

Husk, William Henry, ed. *Songs of the Nativity: Being Christmas Carols, Ancient and Modern*. London: John Camden Hotten, 1867.

Hutchins, Richard. "Christ the Apple Tree." *The Spiritual Magazine* (1761).

"The Jesse Tree." https://www.loyolapress.com/our-catholic-faith/liturgical-year/advent/the-jesse-tree.

Josephus. *Josephus: The Essential Works*. Translated and edited by Paul L. Maier. Grand Rapids: Kregel, 1988.

Kelly, Joseph. *The Origins of Christmas*. Collegeville, MN: Liturgical, 2014.

Keyte, Hugh, and Andrew Parrot, eds. *The New Oxford Book of Carols*. New York: Oxford University Press, 1992.

Kishler, Andrew. Unpublished forthcoming interview. Interviewed by Chris Marchand. September 2018.

Köstenberger, Andreas J. *Encountering John*. Encountering Biblical Studies. Grand Rapids: Baker Academic, 1999.

Lawson-Jones, Mark. *Why Was the Partridge in the Pear Tree? The History of Christmas Carols*. Stroud, UK: History, 2012.

Lewis, C. S. "De Descriptione Temporum: Inaugural Lecture from the Chair of Mediaeval and Renaissance Literature at Cambridge University." Roman Roads Media. https://files.romanroadsstatic.com/old-western-culture-extras/DeDescriptioneTemporum-CS-Lewis.pdf.

———. *Prince Caspian*. New York: HarperTrophy, 2000.

———. *The Silver Chair*. New York: HarperTrophy, 2000.

Lloyd-Jones, Sally. *The Jesus Storybook Bible: Every Story Whispers His Name*. Grand Rapids: Zonderkidz, 2007.

Lupton, Robert D. *Toxic Charity: How Churches and Charities Hurt Those They Help (and How to Reverse It)*. New York: HarperOne, 2011.

Marshall, Taylor. "Yes, Christ Was Really Born on December 25: Here's a Defense of the Traditional Date for Christmas." https://taylormarshall.com/2012/12/yes-christ-was-really-born-on-december.html.

Martimort, A. G., et al. *The Liturgy and Time*. The Church at Prayer 4. Collegeville, MN: Liturgical, 1985.

McGowan, Anne, and Paul F. Bradshaw. *The Pilgrimage of Egeria: A New Translation of the Itinerarium Egeriae with Introduction and Commentary*. Collegeville, MN: Liturgical Academic, 2018.

McKibben, Bill. *Hundred Dollar Holiday*. New York: Simon & Schuster, 1998.

McKnight, George Harley. *St. Nicholas: His Legend and His Role in the Christmas Celebration and Other Popular Customs*. New York: G. P. Putnam's Sons, 1917.

Michlik, Petr, and Gabi Michlik, "Happy Pagan Christmas!" *PostConsumer Reports Podcast*. Interview by Chris Marchand. December, 2018.

Mikkelson, David."The Twelve Days of Christmas: Was the Song 'The Twelve Days of Christmas' Created as a Secret Code by Persecuted Catholics?" https://www.snopes.com/fact-check/twelve-days-christmas/.

Miles, Clement A. *Christmas Customs and Traditions: Their History and Significance*. Mineola, NY: Dover, 2011.

Miller, Daniel, ed. *Unwrapping Christmas*. New York: Oxford University Press, 1993.

Mirth without Mischief: Containing the Twelve Days of Christmas; The Play of the Gaping-Wide-Mouthed-Wadling-Frog; Love and Hatred; The Art of Talking with the Fingers; and Nimble Ned's Alphabet and Figures. London: J. Davenport, 1780.

Nissenbaum, Stephen. *The Battle for Christmas: A Social and Cultural History of Our Most Cherished Holiday*. New York: Vintage, 1997.

Norris, Richard A., Jr., ed. and trans. "The Council of Chalcedon's 'Definition of the Faith.'" In *The Christological Controversy*, 159. Sources of Early Christian Thought. Minneapolis: Fortress, 1980.

Nothaft, C. P. E. "Early Christian Chronology and the Origins of the Christmas Date: In Defense of the 'Calculation Theory.'" *Questions Liturgies* 94.3 (2013) 247–65.

———. "The Origins of the Christmas Date: Some Recent Trends in Historical Research." *Church History* 81.4 (2012) 903–11.

Origen. *Homilies on Leviticus 1–16*. The Fathers of the Church 83. Translated by Gary Wayne Barkley. Washington, DC: Catholic University of America Press, 1990.

Peters, Bosco. "The Incarnation Changes Everything." http://liturgy.co.nz/incarnation-changes-everything?fbclid=IwAR1JB925T9LMU6MEywIn6MyZkIS6utW_o6d1yB q2oA-xw3vVpRtg6kEkP_M.

Pieper, Joseph. *Leisure: The Basis of Culture*. San Francisco, CA: Ignatius, 2009.

Rinaldi, Karen. *It's Great to Suck at Something*. New York: Atria, 2019.

Rocca, Francis X. "Searching for Christianity's Most Sensitive Remnant." *The Star* (Toronto). https://www.thestar.com/news/2007/12/15/searching_for_christianitys_most_sensitive_remnant.html.

Roll, Susan K. Private email correspondence. May 2019.

———. "Some Historical Perspectives." In *Doing December Differently: An Alternative Christmas Handbook*. Glasgow, UK: Wild Goose, 2006.

———. *Toward the Origins of Christmas*. Liturgia Condenda 5. Kampen, Netherlands: Kok Pharos, 1995.

———. Unpublished forthcoming interview. Interviewed by Chris Marchand. April 2019.

Rosenberg, Marshall B. *Nonviolent Communication: A Language of Life*. Encinitas, CA: Puddledancer, 2003.

Rosenstock, Natasha. "Hanukkah Gifts." https://www.myjewishlearning.com/article/hanukkah-gifts/.

Schmemann, Alexander. *For the Life of the World*. Yonkers, NY: St. Vladimir's Seminary, 2010.

Schmidt, Thomas C. "Calculating December 25 as the Birth of Jesus in Hippolytus' *Canon* and *Chronicon*." *Vigiliae Christianae* 69.5 (2015) 542–63.

Sharp, Cecil, et al. "Forfeit Songs; Cumulative Songs; Songs of Marvels and of Magical Animals." *Journal of the Folk-Song Society* 5.20 (1916) 277–96.

Simmons, Kurt M. "The Origins of Christmas and the Date of Christ's Birth." *Journal of the Evangelical Theological Society* 58.2 (2015) 299–324.

Skojec, Jamie. "The Chalking of the Doors." https://onepeterfive.com/the-chalking-of-the-doors-an-epiphany-tradition-explained/.

Steinberg, Leo. *The Sexuality of Christ in Renaissance Art and in Modern Oblivion*. Chicago: University of Chicago Press, 1997.

Stockert, Hal. "The Twelve Days of Christmas: An Underground Catechism." Catholic Information Network. http://www.cin.org/twelvday.html.

Stookey, Laurence Hull. *Calendar: Christ's Time for the Church*. Nashville: Abingdon, 1996.

Sun, Joy. "Should You Donate Differently?" TED talk, 2014. https://www.youtube.com/watch?v=bArH8r8jJ4g

Talley, Thomas J. *The Origins of the Liturgical Year*. Collegeville, MN: Pueblo, 1991.

Tertullian. "Chapter 15: Concerning Festivals in Honour of Emperors, Victories, and the Like. Examples of the Three Children and Daniel." In *On Idolatry*. From Ante-Nicene Fathers 3. Translated by S. Thelwall. Buffalo, NY: Christian Literature, 1885. http://www.newadvent.org/fathers/0302.htm.

Van Loon, Michelle. *Moments and Days: How Our Holy Celebrations Shape Our Faith*. Colorado Springs: NavPress, 2016.

———. Unpublished forthcoming interview. Interviewed by Chris Marchand. July 2018.

Ward, Michael. "C. S. Lewis and the Star of Bethlehem." *Books & Culture* January (2008). https://www.booksandculture.com/articles/2008/janfeb/15.30.html.

———. "C. S. Lewis, Jupiter and Christmas." https://christianthought.hbu.edu/2016/11/19/c-s-lewis-jupiter-and-christmas/.

———. "God the Father of Lights: C. S. Lewis on Christianity and Paganism." *Sacred Architecture* 33 (2006). http://www.sacredarchitecture.org/articles/god_the_father_of_lights_c._s._lewis_on_christianity_and_paganism.

———. *Planet Narnia: The Seven Heavens in the Imagination of C. S. Lewis*. Oxford: Oxford University Press, 2010.

Webber, Robert E., ed. *The Services of the Christian Year*. The Complete Library of Christian Worship 5. Nashville: Star Song, 1994.

Wigglesworth, AmandaEve. *Celebrating the Twelve Days of Christmas: A Family Devotional in the Eastern Orthodox Tradition*. Chesterton, IN: Ancient Faith, 2012.

Yglesias, Matthew. "Can the Cans." https://slate.com/business/2011/12/food-drives-charities-need-your-money-not-your-random-old-food.html.

General Index

Scripture Index